How to Buy and Maintain a Fur Coat

~

How to Buy and Maintain a Fur Coat

A Practical Guide to Luxury

Leslie Goldin
and
Kalia Lulow

Harmony Books/New York

Published by Harmony Books, a division of
Crown Publishers, Inc., 225 Park Avenue South, New York,
New York 10003 and represented in Canada by the
Canadian MANDA Group
HARMONY and colophon are trademarks of
Crown Publishers, Inc.

Manufactured in the United States of America

Library of Congress Cataloging-in-Publication Data
Goldin, Leslie.
How to buy and maintain a fur coat.

Includes index.
1. Fur garments.   I. Lulow, Kalia.   II. Title.
TT525.G63   1986   646'.3   86-12035
ISBN 0-517-56271-5 (pbk.)

10 9 8 7 6 5 4 3 2 1
First Edition

Contents

~

~

To the loving memory of my mother, Mildred Feldman Goldin, to my brother, Alan Goldin, and to my father, Fred Goldin, and sister, Anne Dee Goldin, who are devoted family, friends, and colleagues.

Acknowledgments

~

I WOULD LIKE TO THANK the following people for their expert advice and guidance: Sandy Blye of the American Fur Industry, Sandra Crow, Larry Cowit of Henry Cowit and Sons, Steven Feldman of Harold Feldman Furs, Yale Kramer of Bullock's and Sanger Harris, Michael Kosoff of the Ritz Thrift Shop, Fred Schwartz of the Fur Vault, Ann Valley of Neiman-Marcus, Gil Rothman of Joseph Modell, and my colleagues Evan Karabelas, Joanna Madencis, Joseph Luria, Anne Dee Goldin, Gloria Bassuk, Henry Landman, and Jeff Forman of Goldin-Feldman. I'd also like to give very special thanks to Dr. Russel Taylor for his comments and insights and to Carol Mann for getting the whole thing started.

Preface

~

MANY MORNINGS when my sister, Anne Dee, executive vice-president of Goldin-Feldman, and I travel through the crowded streets of Manhattan's fur district, we look up at a rough brick wall on the side of an old office building and smile. There, a faded sign, painted decades ago, says Bolotkin and Goldin. It's just barely readable; no one else would even notice it, but to us it is a vivid reminder of our past and of our present involvement in forging a new future for the family fur business.

My father, Fred Goldin, started working in the fur district at the age of fourteen. His father, Aaron, had immigrated to this country as a barber, but because barbers worked seven days a week and furriers only six, he switched to the fur business. He brought his young son into the workroom during summers and after school to learn the fur trade.

In 1941, Fred became a partner in his father's company and that same year, after his father's death, he was left to run it on his own. In nineteen forty-two he married my mother, Mildred. Her father, Samuel, and her two brothers, William and Harold, were also furriers. The families and the companies joined forces, becoming Goldin-Feldman.

The fur business boomed after the war, and by the early

seventies it began to change from the small, clublike, private world of family-run, all-male businesses into the multi-billion-dollar fashion industry it is today. It was a change that brought the third and fourth generations of furriers, such as my sister and myself, into the business. Initially, we were steered into other professions. My sister became a well-respected retail clothing buyer and I worked as a speech therapist and teacher of the deaf.

The business was becoming more contemporary and fascinating. Imports made furs an affordable luxury for many younger customers. The average age of a first-time fur buyer dropped from the mid-fifties to the mid-thirties. Leading couture designers from around the world began to create stylish, youthful furs for active women. Women themselves began to buy their own fur coats. The fur business became a challenge full of exciting opportunities, and our father offered us a chance to take part in the new spirit and style by bringing us into the company.

In 1984 we joined forces with Evan Karabelas, who is an integral part of our youthful spirit. I became showroom director, working closely with our individual customers. I love working with these customers and they seem to enjoy having someone to talk with who understands their fears and joy about buying a fur.

The purpose of this book is to pass along what I've learned from listening to my customers' questions and comments. Here is an outline of the basic facts about skins, furs, styles, and maintenance of coats. The purpose is to prepare you to visit a fur shop and establish a good relationship with your furrier. No part of the fur-buying process is as important as your relationship with the person who is selling you the coat. You want honest and sound advice, great service, and dependability. It is my hope that when you learn the basic facts you will feel confident and secure that the coat you buy will give you the best quality and most satisfaction for your dollar, year after year. I want to make buying a fur a pleasure for you.

LESLIE GOLDIN

The Basics

~

Let's face it, walking into a fur salon to buy a coat can be an intimidating experience. You may have lots of questions but are afraid to ask them. You may be nervous about appearing to know too little. You may fear you will be given a fast pitch or, even worse, ignored. If you are not sure of what you are looking for, you may be afraid you'll buy the wrong fur. These are understandable but unnecessary fears; no reputable furrier wants to sell you a coat that is not right for you.

When a customer comes into our showroom I work with her until we find the right coat. I don't think of it as selling but as matchmaking! And now, armed with the information in this book, you can enjoy the same attention. Together we are going to explore everything you need to know about finding the right fur for you. I wish I could give you a pat formula, but there are too many variables. There are no ironclad rules about furs. Prices depend on the market; durability depends in part on overall care and treatment; desirability depends on individual preferences and current styles.

For every if *there is an* and *and a* but. *For example, if you want a mink coat* and *only have nineteen hundred dollars, you may think you can't buy one at all* but, *if you are willing to make some trade-offs, to wait to buy it off-season, to consider a coat made from male instead of female skins, or to purchase an imported dyed mink, there is a larger selection available. What I can give you is a surefire guide that will fine tune your sensibilities about fur so you can decide on the trade-offs you want to make and feel confident in your ability to choose the coat that is best for you.*

If you could go shopping with me, you wouldn't need to know anything more than "I want a fur." Since that's impossible, I want to help you enjoy the quest on your own.

1

The Skins

~

THE BEAUTY OF ANY FUR COAT begins with the skins. No matter how many times I watch our designers transform a bundle of pelts into a finished coat, I am amazed by the skills, the techniques, the magic they possess. They know, from years of experience, what pelts will go together to make a fine fur in an exciting style. They can tell by the look and feel of each skin just how it will work when it is cut and sewn into a coat. To watch them work is to go back to a time when craftsmen everywhere took pride in what they could do with their hands.

Over the years I have learned how to judge the quality of skins and have had the chance to help my customers learn how to evaluate them as well. You, as a consumer, can't know everything about judging a skin's quality, but you can learn enough to give you confidence in your opinion and to enable you to understand the advice of the experts when buying a fur.

When my clients ask me how they can begin to appreciate the difference between a fine skin and one of lesser quality, I give them three guidelines: Use your eyes, your hands, and your shoulders.

If you want to buy a mink, for example, look at and touch as many different mink coats as you can. Notice the contrasts among them. One may have a high luster, a sleek, smooth appearance, and dense fur. Another may seem dull, spikey, and less plush. Feel the leather backs of the skins. On one coat they may be smooth, supple, unblemished; on another they may seem taut, rough, or have thin areas. If you take time to shop around and look at many minks, you will begin to be able to spot the differences in quality. Use this comparison method when you are searching for any fur, not just mink.

Once you have looked at and touched a coat, put it on. You can tell a lot about the quality of the skins by the way a coat feels when you are wearing it. The best skins are lightweight with dense fur and thin leather. Even with heavy furs such as coyote or beaver, the lighter the skins, the finer the quality. We prize these skins because they provide ample warmth and don't strain your shoulders or back. It's like wearing an insulated cloud!

As you can see, understanding the quality of a skin is basically a sensual experience, but there are some solid facts that will help you judge quality, too.

BASIC FACTS

One solid clue to the quality of the skins can be found by checking the label on every fur coat. Since 1952 the Federal Fur Products Labeling Act has made it mandatory for every coat to be identified with the country of origin of the skins and the processing that was done to it—such as shearing, dyeing, color enhancement, or tip dyeing. The label must also indicate whether the fur was made from whole skins or pieces and where it was manufactured. No coat may be given a made-up name for its fur: A rabbit cannot be called lapin; a Canadian marten cannot be called Canadian sable, a muskrat cannot be called mink-dyed muskrat, only dyed muskrat. The American consumer is given more protection from misrepresentation of furs than any other in the world. Canada, for example, requires no such labeling.

Almost all furs, including mink, fox, even chinchilla, are ranched, and the breeding stock has been spread around the globe. Minks, for example, are now raised not only in their native North American climes, but in Scandinavia, China, and even Russia. Sometimes these descendants of the original stock produce quality skins, but that is the exception rather than the rule. Mink from China and Russia is duller, bushier, and redder than American mink. The finest Scandinavian mink skin might be better than an average American one, but the best American mink is always considered superior to one from any other country.

For wild skins, as well as ranched varieties, some countries of origin are superior to others. Sable is an example of a fur that is unique to its country of origin. The Russian variety, both wild and ranched, is the only true sable; and the Russians have made sure it stays that way. Immediately after the Second World War the United States and Russia agreed to exchange breeding pairs of minks for breeding pairs of sable. Today, the Russians raise mink, but you can't find a single sable here. They sent us sterile males and females! What you can find are poor second cousins to the magnificent Russian skins. The so-called Alaskan, Chinese, Canadian, and Norwegian sable are related to Russian sable, but they don't have the delicate texture, warmth, or coloring. The Federal Trade Commission has made it illegal to label any coat sable other than Russian sable, since it is a completely made-up name for another marten.

Lynx is another good example of the importance of the country of origin. Russian lynx is the most expensive. It is rare and very pale in color. The Canadian fur, which is not inexpensive—ranging from $15,000 a coat and up—has a bolder color. American lynx cat is yet another variety. Each one has its virtues and is a fine fur, but they do not have the same quality as Russian lynx and should not cost the same!

Once a skin, either ranched or wild, is chosen to be made into a coat, it must be prepared by being tanned or dressed. The dressing is done by treating the skin with a series of chemicals that, when done properly, will improve the luster and texture of the fur and make the leather durable and easy to tailor.

Once the skins are dressed they are ready to be matched in bundles of skins that can be made into a coat. The art of matching is exacting. It takes an eye for the subtle distinctions of color, fur height, and density to assemble enough pelts to make a coat of uniform quality and color. After the skins for a coat have been matched, they are soaked, stretched, and stapled to a board to prepare them for cutting. There is a right way and a wrong way to do this. Overstretching skins can make a coat less expensive to produce because it takes fewer pelts to make the garment, but it also compromises the durability and overall beauty of the finished product.

Properly prepared and stretched skins will ensure that a coat has an almost voluptuous quality: It folds gently; the fur is dense and even; the leather gives slightly when pulled at the elbow and across the shoulder. A good way to check this on a finished coat is to turn it inside out, lift up the lining, and, using both hands, gently tug on a small section of the leather (about three inches wide). You should be able to feel a little springiness and give.

HOW SKINS ARE ASSEMBLED

As I have said, the quality of any coat depends on the quality of the basic skins used in it and the workmanship that transforms the skins into a fur "fabric." I tell my customers that a little knowledge about these techniques can be a dangerous thing—it is possible to become so opinionated that you don't trust any furrier. But if you are working *with* a furrier, you can use this knowledge to open up a good line of communication. I like it when my customers know enough to ask questions about the coats they try on. I love talking about the way our craftspeople create a fine fur. There are so many variables and so many details to understand.

There are three basic ways in which skins are worked into fabric: let out, skin-on-skin, and pieced. Not all these techniques are right for all styles and all furs. Each method should be carefully and precisely matched with the correct fur. Let-out and skin-on-skin techniques produce very different looks. The narrow striping of a fine mink is the result of the let-out process; the large square panels of a sportier full-skinned mink come from a variation called skin-on-skin construction. Pieced furs are made from the leftover parts of skins that are trimmed off in the production of a let-out or skin-on-skin coat. These heads, paws, gills, and tails are used in low-priced furs.

LET-OUT FURS

Letting-out is a method of cutting a short, rectangular whole stretched skin into narrow diagonal bands of fur and then reassembling the pieces by sewing them into an elongated, thin stripe of fur fabric. In order to make a single stripe from one small skin that is long enough to extend from the top of a coat to the hemline, the furrier must cut the skin into very narrow bands. Three-sixteenths of an inch is the optimum width for mink. Fox, beaver, lynx, coyote, and other heavier, larger furs are also let out, but with much wider diagonal bands. The width of the finished let-out stripe is determined by the size of the original skin and the final length of the coat or jacket. This is why the stripes on a jacket or the sleeves are wider than those on the body of a full-length coat.

You might think that all this cutting weakens the skin, or reduces the surface area of the fur. But nothing is lost in the process. In fact, the cutting and resewing actually make the skin incredibly strong. I tell my customers they could hang from the Empire State Building holding on to a let-out skin.

Once the skins that are going to be used in a coat are let out they are sewn together by joining them to leather strips. On mink and other short-haired furs these strips are about three-sixteenths of an inch wide. Long-haired furs such as fox or lynx require wider leather strips between each pelt. If these furs are not leathered they will not fall evenly or smoothly. Strips of approximately an inch-and-a-quarter width are optimum. Any wider, say an inch and a half to two inches, is a sign that the coat maker has tried to use less fur. On such a coat the leathering will show a lot when you bend your arms or move, or it can be seen when the coat is on a hanger. Even on the finest coats, however, the leather is not entirely invisible.

One time we made a special-order coat from extraordinary skins using one-and-a-quarter-inch leather strips. The finished product was beautiful and costly, but the customer didn't like it because she felt she could see the leather too easily. We made her another coat, using denser skins, which weren't as light and silky but covered the leathering. She was happier and that's what mattered.

The keys to quality in the let-out process are the narrowness of the diagonal bands, the precision with which they are sewn together, and the way in which each long, let-out stripe of fur is attached to the next. To check the quality of any let-out coat, examine the leather side of the skin beneath the lining.

When a let-out fur is finished it should be dense and full enough that the fur covers the seam between the long stripes, and each individual stripe should blend gracefully with the next one. The color distribution across the fabric should be even.

SKIN-ON-SKIN FURS

Skin-on-skin construction is standard on many furs such as sheared nutria and opossum. It is an alternative fashion look for mink and sable. Individual skins are trimmed of the paws, tails, and feet, and when appropriate, the belly or back hairs. The whole skins are anchored onto the pattern board and stapled into place. They are then joined together vertically with leather bands, and they are horizontally sewn directly onto one another.

Each individual skin contains the full color variation of each pelt. Unlike let-out skins, which can be arranged so that all light tones fall across the top of the coat, a skin-on-skin coat will have light and dark fur distributed throughout each pelt; for example, sable is always lighter at the top. If you object to the variation it can be very lightly touched up with a color process called smoking, which lessens the contrast.

One asset of skin-on-skin is that it has a youthful look. We have been making a skin-on-skin Russian golden honey sable for Chloé that is very young-looking and versatile.

Unlike let-out sable, which is very labor intensive and costly to produce, skin-on-skin appeals to a more diverse market. Although sable is still very costly in any form, skin-on-skin makes it more affordable.

PIECED FURS

Pieced furs are made by sewing together the small swatches of fur that are trimmed off whole skins. These trimmings are then sewn together into plates or bolts of fur fabric. The pattern is then cut out of the fur like a cloth coat.

My first fur coat, when I was sixteen, was a pieced mink coat. This coat, with its interesting brown-and-white patchworklike pattern, made me feel elegant. Today, when I design furs for my line called Fur Additions, I use pieced lamb, fox, tanuki, raccoon, and mink in combination with fabric. To obtain all these different types of plates, I comb the New York market and find an infinite variety of furs in an endless choice of colors. Because pieced furs are less expensive than whole skins, they give me a lot of freedom to experiment with colors and styles and to make high-fashion and unusual garments at affordable prices. They are also very useful for linings in wool coats and raincoats.

The economy and the diversity pieced furs offer are the benefits, but they are not always as durable as whole skins. A well-made pieced-fur garment should be reinforced with a China-silk backing that is strengthened with staying—a series of closely placed rows of stitching that help prevent wear and tear along hems and seams, at elbows, and at cuffs.

2

The Fur

~

THE NEXT STEP in gaining confidence so you can enjoy buying a fur coat is to learn a few basics about the choices of fur. Although there is a wide variety available—fifty different types of fur are currently on the market—it is not as overwhelming as it sounds. You will find that there are furs that are long-haired and bushy, and some with long hair that are sleek and flat; there are furs that are short-haired and trim, and others that are much fuller. On one extreme is the extravagant long-haired lynx; on the other, there is the completely flat-furred Persian lamb. In between are many that cannot be so neatly categorized. If you bear in mind that the division of fur into long-haired and short-haired is set up here for your convenience, it will help you sort out all the different types and learn how to evaluate them.

Nature determines whether a fur has long outer hairs—

called guard hairs—that cover the soft underfur, or whether it has outer hairs that are not distinctly longer than the underfur. For example, mink is a short-haired fur; fox is long-haired.

Most furs are left in their natural long- or short-haired form, but sometimes thay are altered to enhance their beauty. Long-haired furs are occasionally plucked of their coarsest and longest guard hairs to give a smooth, even density and coloration to the fur. Both long- and short-haired furs may be sheared, a process that removes all outer hairs and trims the underfur so that it is a soft, even, plush blanket. This is done to create an alternative fashion look; or to make a fur which is not popular in its natural state more commercially desirable or to make it appear more elegant.

Each type of fur has a distinctive look and each offers some advantages and disadvantages. While I think it is important for a consumer to know which she prefers, I often find that a woman has preset ideas about what type of fur she will look best in. And those ideas keep her from finding that truly perfect coat. Every week I meet a new customer who feels that a short-haired fur such as mink is her only option. She thinks that its trim, more conservative look suits her best. Another believes that a flamboyant long-haired fur is the only way to achieve the look of exciting elegance she desires. I try to show the customer that mink can be as traffic-stopping as fox on the right person and in the right style. And a long-haired fur, such as fisher, can be as subtle and refined as mink.

SHORT-HAIRED FURS

The shorter-haired furs are the most popular because they provide warmth, but are not too bulky. Mink is the epitome of this practical elegance. It drapes like fabric and therefore offers more styling options. Other short-haired furs, such as chinchilla, marmot, otter, sable, and weasel, offer the same benefits, with a wide variety of price and style options.

Except for chinchilla, which is very fragile, short-haired furs are generally durable. They do not have long outer guard hairs that easily break off with daily wear and friction. If you are looking for a coat that you can wear every day, to take you from shopping to a swank soirée, short-haired furs may be the answer.

When shopping for short-haired furs, look for the following qualities:

~ The underfur should always be dense and cushiony.

~ The color of the underfur, whether lighter or darker than the outer hairs, should be uniformly distributed.

~ The outer hairs should be smooth to the touch.

~ Lustrous overtones should reflect off the outer hairs.

~ The height and density of the overall fur should be even.

~ The pelts should be arranged so that the finest ones are on the front of the garment and the thickest, most cushiony are along the bottom.

LONG-HAIRED FURS

With their dramatic, beautifully colored guard hairs, longer-haired furs such as coyote can be real showstoppers. Nothing has the stunning impact of a Russian lynx or a fisher. Tanuki or beaver offers high style with real versatility, warmth, and durability. Other furs that have medium to long hair include badger, fitch, fox, marten, and nutria.

Long-haired furs do have some disadvantages. All long-haired furs shed—some minimally, others a great deal. Some are extremely vulnerable to friction and daily wear and tear. You cannot expect to sit on a fox coat while you ride to work and have it survive even one season without some matting, worn spots, and loss of guard hairs.

When you are shopping for a long-haired fur, look for the following qualities:

~ Guard hairs should always be silky.
~ Guard hairs should be evenly distributed over the coat and of uniform appearance in length and density.
~ The color pattern on guard hairs should be arranged so that the skins create a pleasing color pattern throughout the coat.
~ Guard hairs should not be broken, matted, or thinning.
~ The underfur should be very soft and create a resilient cushion.
~ The coat should be assembled so that the seams between the pelts are covered by the natural fall of the fur. No fur should be snagged within the stitches.

NATURAL VERSUS DYED FURS

The incredible variety of fur colors now available is the result of new techniques in animal husbandry used to raise farm-bred furs and of methods of dyeing and color enhancement. Both natural and dyed furs have special assets, although it is true that skins with the most beautiful natural fur are not dyed. Always check the label for color information. The law requires that a fur be identified as natural or color enhanced.

There are three categories of natural fur colors: ranch colors, which are farm-bred furs in Mother Nature's original shades; mutation colors, which are developed by crossbreeding farm-bred furs; and wild fur colors. The advent of natural mutation colors, particularly, has created many new shades of fox, mink, rabbit, and other furs. When we use dye, we increase the color selection even more. Dyeing is used to create a fashion look or simply to make a less expensive fur appear more costly than it really is.

The consumer needs to know about dyed furs because the process does have trade-offs. Some dyeing techniques weaken the leather and alter the durability of a fur.

Fortunately, the art of dyeing fur has come a long way. The chemicals used are much gentler than they used to be, and the problems of leather damage and fading colors have largely been eliminated. However, no reputable furrier can guarantee that a dyed fur will not change color, because all fur oxidizes over time, but the fading should be gradual.

DIP OR VAT DYEING

Furs that are dipped or vat dyed are submerged into coloring agents. Not only does the fur—both guard hairs and underfur—become uniform in tone, but the leather itself is dyed, which dries it out. Dipping fur dulls the color and shortens the wearing life of the coat. A mink that is dip dyed solid black will wear out sooner than a natural brown-black ranch mink, because the dyeing robs the skin of oils. Only lesser-quality mink skins are used in coats that are to be dip dyed. Note that there is no such thing as natural pitch-black mink, and if it is black mink you want, then dyeing is your only option.

To check if a coat is dyed, you can always look at the leather under the lining. Dyed leather will uniformly have a bluish black color. Leather that is creamy white with bluish black stripes along the seams of leather stripping between the fur has not been dyed. The stripes are added to keep the pale leather at the seams from showing through the fur, and they do not compromise the leather or the durability.

Dip dyeing of fur is not always a sign of poor quality, except with mink. Sheared beaver, lamb, or nutria is often dip dyed in a rainbow of colors to make fashion statements. The incredible colors—from teal blue to scarlet red—are used to enhance those furs and make them seem more glamorous.

In the entire New York fur market, there are only a few places where furs are dyed. We go to them with the color swatches that our designers like Chloé give us, and then we look through their vast catalogue of colors, trying to find the right dyes to match this season's high-fashion colors as previewed in the Paris ready-to-wear and couture shows.

COLOR- OR DYE-ADDED

Another method of color enhancement is known as color-added, and furs that have undergone this process should be so labeled. This is a very mild form of dyeing done during the dressing of the skin. It does not affect the strength of the leather and serves to improve the color without removing gradations of tone or the contrast between top hairs and underfur. Even very fine coats may have this done to accentuate a certain tone or color, to brighten up the sheen on a fur, or to make the color distribution or pattern blend well together. Many long-haired furs such as fox and raccoon, as well as rabbit, are often color-added.

Color-added furs look very natural, and you should not be able to tell except by reading the label that this has been done to a fur.

FEATHER OR TIP DYEING

This most moderate of all dyeing methods can be used to bring a silvery shimmer to the guard hairs on minks, foxes, and raccoons. Highlights are tenderly, and literally, applied with a feather.

BLEACHING

Some inexpensive minks and rabbits are bleached to give them that stark whiteness some people prize. Natural, pure-white furs such as white mink, ermine, and rabbit have a depth of tone which bleaching cannot re-create, but it can often come close. The chemicals used do weaken the leather and lessen the durability. We never bleach our furs, and I recommend you stay away from bleached skins, too.

BRIGHTENING

Brightening is a kind of bleaching that is always done to raccoon—to make the tips of the longest, silvery guard hairs more lustrous and more brightly white or silver—and to white fox, mink, and rabbit. It doesn't dry the leather or hurt the fur and is really a plus.

PATTERN DYES

Some furs such as mole, rabbit, and sheared beaver are often dyed to look like leopard and other now-outlawed and endangered furs. All patterns should, of course, look as natural as possible. The colors should be blended, the tones varied. Avoid furs that have a pattern that is too rigid; they will look too unnatural.

BLUSH DYEING

Blushing is a technique used on white and black-cross furs such as white mink and white (shadow) fox to give a soft, golden beige tone to the underfur. It creates the illusion that the white outer hairs are even whiter; I think they have a look of freshly fallen snow.

TOUCH-UP

After you buy a coat you may want your furrier to add color to the collar edges, lapels, or cuffs. We do recommend this on brown (lunaraine) and gray (lutecia) minks because the difference in color between the underfur and outer hair is great. Wherever you bend this type of fur—as at a collar edge—the lighter fur looks thin and the underhair shows through and appears worn. It isn't, but the color contrast creates this illusion, and darkening the underfur alleviates the problem.

3

The Variety

~

EVEN THOUGH I have been around fur all my life, it wasn't until I began working in my family's showroom that I appreciated just how wide a selection of furs there is. I know how you feel when you enter a store and are confronted by a cloud of colors. The coats seem to blur together. Is that a silver fox? Or a silver raccoon? A sheared beaver or a sheared nutria? What makes one mink more expensive than another? What are the differences between all the raccoon coats crowded on one rack? Who can tell?

I have assembled profiles of the furs most customers are curious about. Once you read the descriptions and begin to comparison shop, you will be able to discriminate between the various levels of quality and train your eye to recognize the difference between the subtle pattern of stone marten and the dramatic stripe of fitch. You will become aware that a cross fox is a delicate fur, while tanuki, which has similar coloring, is much sturdier. Even the vast range of minks will become familiar. Exploring the variety is part of the joy of shopping for a fur.

I often compare looking for a fur to buying a car. When you start the process, all of a sudden you notice every blue sedan on the street. You check them out, compare, ask questions. You become streetwise. That's what should happen to you as you begin to look for a fur. If you see a woman in a beautiful coat, ask her what type of fur it is and where she got it. She won't mind. She will be proud and complimented. She probably went through similar insecurities, although she now appears totally sophisticated and confident. Also, look through all the fashion magazines to see what styles and furs are being featured this season. You may not want to buy a fur that is as extreme as some you'll see, but you will get a good idea of current trends, styles, and prices.

The varieties of furs you'll become acquainted with are described briefly in the following sections.

SHORT-HAIRED FURS

CHINCHILLA

Chinchilla, the fur of starlets and queens, is very lightweight yet warm. Nothing has its tactile thrill. At the beginning of the century, chinchilla became so popular that there was a threat of extinction. Today, it is raised as a ranched fur in the United States.

Natural chinchilla has dark underfur with slate blue or silver top hair. Many new mutation colors have been bred; but they all have the distinctive contrast between the top hairs and the underfur. The chinchilla itself is a small rodent, so the skins are difficult to work with and very fragile. It takes many pelts to make a coat, and the craftsmen who have the expertise to create these fashions are highly skilled. It is expensive but the price has gone down because there is not much demand for it. These days a chinchilla coat might be as little as eight thousand dollars or as high as the sky!

ERMINE

Long considered the fur of royalty, ermine is a winter weasel with unique pure-white hair and a soft, silky texture. The guard hairs are smooth and fall over a pillow of thick underfur. Very sensitive to light, ermine oxidizes, or yellows, over time. It is rarely found on the market.

MARMOT

Russian and Chinese marmot, which are the best, offer a budget-conscious consumer a quality alternative to mink. In its natural state, marmot is bluish before hibernation and yellowish after, but when the fur is dyed dark brown or black it looks like mink, although it is much coarser to the touch. Dyeing shortens its wearing life, but even so, a marmot coat will last about ten years with good care. With the advent of popularly priced minks there is not a big demand for this fur and it is rarely seen in today's market.

MINK

Mink, the great American fur, accounts for almost seventy-five percent of all furs purchased in the United States. With the advent of sophisticated ranching techniques many new mutation colors have been created. Today, mink is suitable for the most formal, the most sporty, the most conservative, and the most daring fur buyer. People love mink because it drapes like fabric, is light yet warm, wears like iron, has great color variety, doesn't shed, lasts for years, and can be worn from early fall through early spring.

There are basically two types of farm-bred minks available—ranched and mutation.

Ranch mink, the name applied to brown-black natural mink, has a deep luster, a slightly silvery glisten to the top hairs, and is velvety soft. It appears black but if you look at it closely you will see it is dark brown with some white hairs. There are various trade names for ranched mink: Blackglama is the designation for American skins; Majestic is the Canadian name; and Saga tells you the ranch skins came from Scandinavia.

Mutation mink designates any fur color that is the product of crossbreeding. Emba is the American trademark; Saga and Majestic apply to mutation, as well as ranched furs from Scandinavia and Canada. These minks range in tones from pale white and beige to blue gray and brown. Every year new and wonderful colors come on the market, including wild-type reddish brown mink, now bred on ranches. Some of the industry names for the colors include: black-cross, white fur with black markings; lunaraine, ranging from light brown to true deep brown; tourmaline, a soft beige; autumn haze, an almost pink beige; blue iris, a blue gray; azurine, a soft, pale blue gray; and arcturus, an off-white with a brownish stripe. To make matters even more confusing, in addition to these general names many manufacturers have their own made-up names for the specific colors. They are not indicative of any unique color, but only of the manufacturer's marketing strategy. My advice is, learn to assess the quality behind the lables.

Male versus Female Mink   Male mink is not necessarily inferior in quality to female mink. As a matter of fact, years ago male skins were prized for their larger size and their very dense, heavy fur. Now we feel the male skins are less desirable because of their extra weight. To create a full-length split male mink coat, the furrier cuts each let-out male pelt in half lengthwise—creating two pelts—before assembling the coat. Male pelts are also worked using what is called the reset technique. Used to make jackets, this technique has been perfected so you cannot tell the difference between a reset male and a let-out female jacket. To achieve this, the pelt is sliced diagonally (as a female pelt is cut). Then every other band of fur is sewn together into two separate let-out lengths of skin. From each male pelt, the furrier obtains two stripes of fur fabric.

Using male skins is more labor intensive than using female skins, but because each skin is less expensive and there is more fur per skin and less demand for the product, the coat should be less expensive. The male skins may be your best choice if you want a fuller look, and they are very useful if you need an extra-long coat, since each skin can be let out into a longer stripe than can a smaller female skin. If you like a particular coat of male mink, there is no reason not to consider it a smart purchase.

Mink coats are available in a huge range of prices depending on the quality and quantity of skins used and cost to manufacture and sell. Some coats manufactured in the Far East sell for half the cost of an American-made coat. These coats, which used to be inferior in basic fur and in workmanship, are improving all the time. Prices for imported and domestic coats can dip as low as fifteen hundred dollars and go as high as twenty-five thousand dollars. There is a mink coat available for almost every budget and every taste.

MOLE

A soft, dull gray, short-haired fur, mole is neither durable nor particularly beautiful in its natural state. When dyed deep brown or black the velvety fur makes it most suitable for coats, vests, shawls, or jackets.

Mole is not very warm, but quite inexpensive.

OTTER

Otter was once a very fashionable fur, but is rarely used these days. Many species are now endangered and protected by law, although American and Canadian otter are not. Otter is a sleek fur, brown in color, with a very heavy, dense underfur. Traditionally it was plucked or sheared, but now it is also left full length. Because of its slightly coarse, rugged look, it is a favorite for men's fur coats. It is extremely durable, lasting almost as long as mink, and very warm. Otter is a medium-priced fur, comparable in cost to raccoon. It offers many seasons of wear.

SABLE

Sable, the fur of the czars, is the most luxurious and most costly of all furs. All true sable is trapped wild or ranched in Russia.

Wild sable is prized for its glistening silver-tipped outer hairs. The colors range from the warm golden and honey browns to deep dark browns. There is a subtle variety of color within any one sable pelt, and when sewn into a coat this creates a gentle pattern of light and dark tones.

Ranched sables, which are becoming more and more common, rarely have the silvery glisten to them, and when they do they are quite expensive. Their basic color tones range from deep, rich browns to brown blacks. The difference in tone between the underfur and the outer hairs is less pronounced in ranched skins than in the wild fur.

The art of creating a sable coat is highly specialized and very labor intensive. According to Steven Feldman, "Matching and joining sable is very difficult. It takes about seventy sable skins to make a standard-length coat, but you may have to examine a thousand skins to find the seventy that go together in one coat. Then, once you have chosen the skins, you must create a smooth, even fabric." To do that, a furrier goes through a painstaking variation of the let-out technique that demands keen sensitivity.

Sometimes you will see a coat labeled as blended sable. This means that it was constructed from skins that were not perfectly color matched and had a gentle dye added to give it a uniform color distribution.

Male versus Female Sable   Unlike mink, male and female sables are used together in the same coat. Male sable is somewhat thicker than female; however, the variation in hair density on any one skin, male or female, is quite great. An overall even density is achieved by arranging the female pelts so that their thickest sections abut the thinnest parts of the male pelts. This intricate arrangement of furs is very important for the overall drape and texture of any sable coat. An even distribution of fur density is one of the signs of superior quality.

Sable is expensive. Not only is it relatively rare, there being less than one hundred and fifty thousand skins a year available from the Russian government; but it is also in great demand. Sable coats can easily cost fifty thousand dollars or more at elegant retail furriers. The most expensive coat we ever made was a natural dark sable. It retailed for one hundred and fifty thousand dollars.

WEASEL

The weasel family includes a wide variety of furs— marten, mink, ermine, and sable are all weasels. But when a fur is called a weasel—as opposed to any of those other designations—the name refers to an inferior, less durable cousin. Weasels are found in many countries. Each variety has its own coloration, which is affected by both season and geography. You can identify weasel because it has shorter hair than mink and its natural fur is brown with yellow and beige tones throughout. To make it seem more like its distinguished relatives, weasel is often dyed dark brown or black.

This is a very economical fur, costing far less than even an inexpensive mink. It offers style and can be attractive, but it will last only about three to five years.

LONG-HAIRED FURS

BADGER

The badger is a very sturdy long-haired fur, often used in men's coats. Like raccoon it wears well for years and years, but badger is very heavy and often constructed with leather banding between the pelts to make it lighter on the shoulders, which reduces the durability of the coat. The color varies, depending on its origin, but is generally a light yellow-brown marked with touches of gray and beige guard hairs. Badger is inexpensive, since there is not much demand for it. You will get a lot of coat for your fur dollar.

BEAVER

Natural beaver is the fur of choice for many young customers because it is sporty, durable, and prices begin at fifteen hundred dollars. The most expensive and rarest beaver is pale blonde, but most beaver ranges from dark to light brown.

COYOTE

Coyote, the modern replacement for the endangered wolf, has an abundance of guard hairs and dense underfur and often has quite subtle markings. It is a slightly coarse-textured fur with a gray and tan tone to the under hair and an off-white tone of the guard hair. It is a durable fur but when the pale guard hairs wear away you see the gray underhair and this makes worn spots very apparent. Somewhat heavy to wear, its big pluses are warmth and durability. As demand increases, coyote is getting more expensive, but it is still considered a medium-priced fur. For those who want a dramatic fur more durable than most fox coats, coyote offers a beautiful alternative.

FISHER

This magnificent fur ranges in color from rich deep browns to pale browns and is increasingly being appreciated for its luxury and its practicality. Fisher is the luxury fur of the eighties. The high sheen of the thick guard hairs and dense warm blanket of underfur are truly beautiful. Each skin is lighter in color at the top and when let out the whole coat should have a gradual deepening of tone from shoulder to hemline. Furthermore, it is durable and shed-resistant. A Canadian cousin of the sable, fisher, like mink, is softest and lightest in weight when made from female skins. This fur, which has a subtle but very luxurious look, is well suited to anyone who desires a coat that fits into every social occasion. It has a deceptively casual appearance. We find that the rarity of fine skins and its warmth and durability mean the coats sell quickly regardless of cost. The most expensive fisher, in a rich deep brown, can cost more than fifty thousand dollars in a full-length coat. Others may be less than twenty thousand dollars, depending on your source.

FITCH

Fitch has long hairs but is a flat fur. It is a good choice for the woman who wants an interesting alternative to mink. The best fitch has blue-white underhair, with a sharply contrasting layer of dark guard hairs. When let out, fitch is a distinctive fur characterized by strong black-and-white stripes. When done skin-on-skin, fitch is not striped but creates a large interesting pattern.

FOX

Fox is a wonderfully diverse fur, available in an enormous variety of colors and prices. It can be as magnificent as a Russian lynx, as sporty as raccoon, or as arresting as a fisher. Although fox has a reputation for being fragile, and sheds, some varieties are more durable than others. Fox will last for many seasons with the proper care and cleaning. It is not generally thought of as a practical fur for everyday wear, and most people hesitate to buy it as their only coat, but this caution is unnecessary. If your spirit yearns for fox, don't deny it. You only live once.

One alternative that many furriers are suggesting these days is the use of fox trim on the body of another fur. For example, a ranch mink coat with a silver fox collar and lapel makes a beautiful garment. You can enjoy the feel and look of fox around your face with the durability and economy of mink on the rest of the coat. A drawback is that the trim is usually put on in the places that wear out most easily. You also have to make sure the coat doesn't look like it has been remodeled.

Fox is available in many natural and dyed colors. New mutation colors are created every year. Golden Island is a truly rare golden red; Fawn is a costly soft beige; and Arctic Marble is an expensive white fur with touches of gray. Dyed fox is also available. Among the most popular choices are blush, white with beige underfur, and crystal, silver blue with gold undertones. Each of these tones is given a name by the breeder or manufacturer, but you don't need to memorize their marketing lingo. Stick with the basics and the furrier will help you find the right color for you.

Blue Fox   A Scandinavian ranched fox, this is distinguished by its pale gray or blue-white cast. It offers warmth and glamor but sheds and is very delicate. Silver blue fox is a cross between silver and blue fox. It is probably the most durable fox and is often dyed by adding a golden undertone to create Crystal fox.

Cross Fox   This unusual patterned fur, a combination of red and gray fox, has a distinctive black-cross pattern throughout. It is called silver cross fox when it is produced by crossing silver and red fox. It is a fragile and expensive fox, suitable for high-style coats and jackets not worn on a daily basis.

Platinum   With its light white tones it is a rare mutation fur. Its beautiful color is in the head and paws, so unlike other fox coats, these parts are used in the finished garment.

Red Fox   One of the less expensive foxes, red fox is often used in sporty jackets and worked in with leather or cloth as well as full-length coats. You can tell a fine red fox by the density of the fur and the uniformity and clarity of the coloring. The most desirable fox has less white in its underfur.

Silver Fox This is one of the most expensive and most durable natural fox. A ranched mutation fur like platinum fox, it has a true silver tone to its guard hairs and a silver and brown black accent in the underfur. Not only does it wear better than other foxes, but it also sheds less. Silver Shadow has a basic white undercolor with shadings of silver tones on the guard hairs.

White Fox A magnificent stark white, often bleached or brightened to enhance its color, white fox is prone to yellowing with time and is very delicate, but it creates an impact that is unexcelled.

Fox, more than almost any other fur, can be inexpensive or fabulously pricey. So much depends on the styling and the quality of the basic pelts. Now that they are ranched and some are manufactured offshore they may be affordable and beautiful. Furriers have contrived methods of construction that allow them to produce fox jackets using fewer skins. These low-priced items are not equal in beauty to their refined, expensive relatives. On the other hand, the rare mutation varieties can cost thousands of dollars more than mink. These are manufactured by the highest paid craftsmen. If it's a fox you want, a fox you can have, at almost any price.

LYNX

Lynx is one of the most precious and beautiful of all furs. Its soft guard hairs cover a dense pillow of very soft underfur. The finest pelts are very pale white and have very subtle, dramatic coloring on the guard hairs.

There are several varieties of lynx. Each is a fine fur and offers a wide variety in price and coloring. All lynx are wild and the price depends on the availability of skins.

Russian Lynx The quite infrequent exports of this fur are controlled by the Russian government. Each year only so many skins can be found that match up well enough to create a top-quality coat. The creamy white underfur is touched with very beige markings in subtle spotted patterns. The long guard hairs are flat, making it sleeker than Canadian lynx. This is a very expensive fur, with coats priced around seventy-five thousand dollars. Maxmillian, furrier to the stars, offers a lynx for a quarter of a million dollars.

Canadian Lynx This is a close second in beauty to the Russian lynx. It has slightly bolder colors with longer hair and a more pronounced contrast between the underfur and the guard hairs. When purchased at a fine retail store, it can cost around thirty thousand dollars.

Montana and American Cat Lynx These are the least subtle of lynx furs, with a strong spotted contrast between the reddish guard-hair colors and the white underfur. These contrasts can be worked to create a vivid and interesting pattern along the collar and shoulders of a coat. The shorter, flatter fur suits those who want a trimmer-looking lynx. American and Montana lynx both cost less than Russian but retail for fifteen thousand dollars and up.

Bobcat When compared to a Russian lynx, this is another breed of cat altogether. This relatively inexpensive fur is predominately red-toned with black hair tips. The belly hair is white. The overall hair is much flatter than Russian, Canadian, or American lynx and less sumptuous, but young and lively in appearance.

In general, however, most lynx is quite warm and light, and although fragile, with proper care it can last up to eight years.

MARTEN

Marten is a member of the same family as sable, but that is where the similarities end. In and of itself, marten is a wonderful, varied fur that offers beauty, durability, and warmth. They are medium long-haired furs and have a wonderful texture and luxurious quality. There are three types of marten on the market: American, baum, and stone. Each one comes in unique colors suited only to certain people.

American Marten   This is the least expensive variety and offers good durability and warmth. It is characterized by very long guard hairs and a particularly thick blanket of underfur. Sometimes the guard hairs are plucked to create a smooth finish. The colors range from a deep bluish brown and brown black to a pale yellow with orange tones.

When made into a coat it can be worked in long, thin let-out stripes or in sportier and wider skin-on-skin squares.

Baum Marten   This is a softer and more lustrous fur than its American cousin. A native of Europe and the Himalayan mountains, the fur is a taupey green brown. Not everyone can wear it well, because it can give a greenish cast to the skin. Its gill, or neck, is orange. Baum marten is often dyed to resemble sable. A fine coat can cost up to thirty thousand dollars.

Stone Marten This is the most popular of the martens and has much more exotic colorings than its relatives. The underfur is a blushing beige or blue white and the guard hairs have a soft, taupe-beige cast. Its gill, or neck, is white. When worked into a coat it produces a blend of dark and light fur.

The stone marten is the warmest, most durable, and the most costly marten.

MUSKRAT

Common to swamp lands all over this country, muskrat is often used as a sheared fur. When left in its natural state, it is long-haired with thick guard hairs and a dense underfur. Once it was made as a let-out coat and dyed to imitate mink. Now, with inexpensive minks available, this is no longer done.

Muskrat is strong and hearty with distinctive stripes of silver and black. Because it is not in great demand, muskrat is inexpensive and plentiful.

NUTRIA

This South American rodent, out of style for many years, is making a big comeback because of its durability and warmth. A cousin of the beaver, it is now ranched in the southern United Sates. Often it is used as a dyed, sheared fur. Its long, glossy brown guard hairs cover a dense brown layer of underfur.

Still price worthy, nutria wears moderately well and is

warm. It is a practical alternative and can be styled skin-on-skin or let out.

OPOSSUM

The opossum is a long-haired silver gray fur when it is from America, a short-haired plush fur when from Australia.

The American opossum is moderately durable and very warm. It is often used for coat linings or sporty jackets, and cost of an opossum is low.

Australian opossum is a pleasing blue gray color when natural. It is, however, frequently dyed or sheared. It costs more than American opossum but lasts almost twice as long.

RABBIT

Rabbit is now ranched and is available in an enormous variety of colors and in both long- and short-haired furs. It is frequently dyed, sheared, or plucked to imitate more expensive furs. But no matter how it is presented, it is not durable, lasting only a few seasons. Unsheared, it sheds badly.

The cost is low, and the look and feel can be attractive, so it may be just the fur for an impulse purchase.

Lapin, or French rabbit, is usually sheared or corduroyed and dyed beautifully. But, remember, it's still just rabbit with an accent.

RACCOON

Raccoon is no longer worn only by Ivy Leaguers at football games, but is now one of the most popular furs for both men and women. It is beautiful, warm, durable, and absolutely perfect in any social situation—from shopping to the opera. The best raccoon has shimmery silver-and-black highlights on its long guard hairs and a thick, full cushion of warm brown and gray underfur. It should always have brightener added to enhance its silvery tone.

Raccoon is more durable and heavier than many furs.

Raccoon is a medium- to low-priced fur, depending on the style and where you buy it. When comparison shopping, notice that less expensive raccoons have thinner underfur and fewer silvery tones to their flatter guard hairs.

SKUNK

A flashy, bold, long-haired fur, with a pronounced black and white stripe, skunk is used in high-fashion coats and jackets. The South American skunk, known as zorina, has flatter and glossier guard hairs. When sewn into a coat, the white stripes against the blue black fur should appear as an accent.

Both North American and South American skunk are inexpensive and warm, with moderate durability, but have an unpleasant odor when wet, so are rarely found on the market.

TANUKI

The Japanese relative of the raccoon, tanuki is a relatively new fur on the market. It offers all the advantages of raccoon plus a more elegant, warmer look that suits the hair, skin, and eye color of some people. The fur is red gold or blue gold with black-tipped guard hairs running throughout. When the coat is constructed, the cross markings are often matched up to create a beautiful pattern across the shoulder blades. The beauty and fancy of the fur are in its interesting patterns.

Tanuki is more expensive than raccoon because it is imported and somewhat rarer. A premium tanuki would be lightweight, warm, a clear vivid gold in color, with a minimum of red tones, and made from the finest, smallest female skins. Therefore it commands a premium price. But it is generally a medium-priced fur, selling for between thirty-five hundred and five thousand dollars. When its cost is viewed in terms of its long life expectancy, it becomes a very practical expenditure.

LAMB

There are many different types of lamb, each one with its own unique properties. It can be long-haired and lush, tightly curled and delicate, inexpensive or very costly.

BROADTAIL LAMB

The rarest and most expensive lamb, it is made from the skins of stillborn Russian and Turkish lambs. Characterized by its tight moiré pattern and thin skin, broadtail lamb does not wear well and is not warm, but is strikingly beautiful. It is used for suits as well as coats and jackets, and even long gowns, because it drapes like fine fabric.

PROCESSED BROADTAIL

This is an imitation from Argentina of the classic broad-tail. Fur ranchers have been able to produce a skin that is more durable and less expensive. The broadtail-like moiré pattern is created by shearing the fur, not by the use of stillborn lambs.

PERSIAN LAMB

Also called Karakul, Swakara, or Bukhara, but whatever the name, this is a handsome, durable fur that has gone in and out of vogue over the decades. As a consequence, it is often very inexpensive.

Most black Persian coats are dyed, but its natural color ranges from white to gray and brown.

MONGOLIAN LAMB

This is a distinctive long-haired lamb with a fun and frivolous look, usually left in its natural off-white tone and used in sporty jackets and coats. It can be dyed with bright, clear colors and sewn with the leather side out. The best Mongolian lamb is wavy, never frizzy, and the leather is smooth and well-dressed.

SHEARED FURS

Sheared furs, whether from long- or short-haired skins, are created by removing all guard hairs and part of the under-fur for a very soft, velvety, compact fur. The process of shearing makes the coat more susceptible to water damage from rain or snow (except for treated mouton) and more easily damaged by daily wear. With yearly cleaning and careful daily maintenance, sheared fur can have a long, attractive life.

There are two signs of quality to look for in any sheared fur:

~ Uniformity of shearing. The density and height of the hairs should not vary at all across the entire coat.
~ Invisibility of the seams between pelts. Don't buy a sheared coat that parts at the seams; it will wear badly and look old before its time.

Any fur could, theoretically, be sheared, even mink. There are five varieties that are most commonly sheared:

BEAVER

Beaver is the most frequently sheared fur. Until recently beaver was rarely sold in its natural state. A sheared beaver is a beautiful brown with a shadowy stripe but can be dyed any color. It is a good buy in jackets or full-length coats, although it may become matted when wet and must be cleaned once a year. Many customers have the idea that beaver is a fur for grandmas, but that's an old notion. With the right styling, beaver can be fabulous.

MOUTON

Mouton is sheared lamb, and an attractive, price-worthy fur. The classic mouton is an evenly sheared, very dense, dyed brown fur. It is processed to make it water repellent, which makes it more durable than other sheared furs. These days it is available in all kinds of fashion colors and styles. Its moderate price and youthful appearance make it a great first fur for those with a casual lifestyle.

MUSKRAT

Sheared and dyed to look like more expensive furs such as mink or seal, muskrat is an inexpensive fur with warmth and durability, and it is a good buy.

NUTRIA

This is a ranched fur that makes a lightweight coat. It's our choice for fur linings in men's and women's raincoats and wool coats because of its weightlessness and warmth. The natural color is a medium brown, but it is often blended to a deeper brown or dyed black. It remains warm and is relatively durable if it is cared for and cleaned annually.

SHEARLING

Shearling is also sheared lamb, but unlike mouton, it is left slightly longer and less compact. It is often left in its natural creamy color, and its leather is sueded. It's usually fashioned into brown suede coats that have the fur on the inside as a lining.

Overall, sheared furs are a great choice if you want high-fashion style and colors or love the incredibly soft feeling. Generally, the shearing adds to the cost, even when it is the only way to transform some furs.

ENDANGERED SPECIES

The fur industry is very carefully regulated in the United States and must observe strict laws governing the raising or trapping and the sale of fur-bearing animals. Many countries have no legislation to protect endangered species.

If you buy a fur in Asia or Europe that is made from an endangered animal, it will be confiscated by Canadian or United States Customs. You cannot even sell an old used fur made from an endangered species. Some furriers have such coats tucked away in their vaults, but they can only use them to repair existing garments.

The animal furs once commonly used in coats but now banned in the United States and Canada are: jaguar, ocelot, mountain lion, cheetah, several species of South American otter, giant otter, leopard, most primates, wolf, harp seal, volcano rabbit, Formosan yellow-throated marten, and many African deer, antelopes, and gazelles.

Fur Facts

SHORT-HAIRED FURS

	COST	COLOR	DURABILITY
CHINCHILLA	$6,000–$20,000	slate blue guard hairs; dark silver underfur; mutation colors	8–10 yrs.
ERMINE	*	pure white	approx. 10 yrs.
MARMOT	$1,000–$7,000	bluish brown before hibernation, yellow after; usually dyed brown or black	5–10 yrs.
MINK	$1,500–$25,000	enormous range of colors—from pale whites and beiges to deep brown-blacks	15–20 yrs.
MOLE	$2,000–$7,500	gray in natural state; usually dyed, often deep brown or black	5–7 yrs.
OPOSSUM Australian	$1,000–$3,000	yellow-gray to blue-gray; frequently dyed	10 yrs.
OTTER	$3,000–$8,000	brown	10–15 yrs.
SABLE	$15,000–$150,000	golden honey to deep dark brown	15 yrs.
WEASEL	*	natural fur is brown with yellow and beige tones; usually dyed brown or black	3–5 yrs.

*Price depends on availability
†**VW**—*very warm;* **W**—*warm;* **NW**—*not warm*

Texture	Warmth†	Maintenance
silky dense underfur	**VW**	fragile skins; not an everyday fur; clean every 2 years
long, thick, silky guard hairs; soft underfur	**W**	avoid excess exposure to light—oxidizes over time; not an everyday fur
coarse, thick outer hairs	**W**	standard daily care; clean every 2 years; guard hairs very breakable
very soft, silky outer hairs with high luster	**VW**	standard daily care; clean every 2 years
no nap, very soft	**NW**	avoid rain; very fragile; clean as needed; annual summer storage
plush short hairs	**VW**	standard daily care; clean every 2 years; annual summer storage
coarse, thick outer hairs with high luster	**VW**	standard daily care; clean every 2 years
very soft guard hairs; cushiony, dense underfur	**W**	standard daily care; clean every 2 years
very soft, short outer hairs	**W**	standard daily care; clean every 2 years

LONG-HAIRED FURS

	Cost	Color	Durability
BADGER	$3,000–$12,000	white and yellow-brown underfur with gray and beige markings	15–20 yrs.
BEAVER	$1,500–$7,000	natural fur brown with yellow and beige tones; usually dyed brown or black	10–15 yrs.
COYOTE	$2,000–$7,000	gray and tan underhair; off-white guard hairs	5–8 yrs.
FISHER	$9,000–$45,000	ranges from pale to rich deep brown	10–15 yrs.
FITCH	$3,000–$14,000	blue-white or yellow underhair with sharply contrasting dark guard hairs	8–10 yrs.
FOX			
Blue	$1,200–$6,000	pale gray with blue-white cast	5–10 yrs.
Cross	$5,000–$20,000	combination of red and gray fox with black-cross pattern	5–10 yrs.
Red	$1,500–$8,000	red with white tones	5–10 yrs.
Silver	$5,000–$20,000	silver guard hairs; silver and brown-black accent to underfur	8–12 yrs.
(Shadow) White	$2,000–$7,500	stark white	5–10 yrs.
LYNX			
Russian	$25,000–$250,000	creamy white underfur with beige markings	8–10 yrs.
Canadian	$6,000–$20,000	creamy white underfur with beige markings but bolder contrasts than Russian	5–8 yrs.
Montana	$4,500–$20,000	reddish guard hairs; white underfur	5–8 yrs.
Bobcat	$1,000–$8,000	red tones with black tips; white belly hair	5–8 yrs.

TEXTURE	WARMTH	MAINTENANCE
heavy, thick guard hairs; dense underfur	**W**	standard daily care; clean every 2 years
thick, lustrous guard hairs; soft underfur	**VW**	standard daily care; clean every 2 years
very long, silky guard hairs; dense underfur	**VW**	standard daily care; clean every 2 years
fine, silky, thick, moderately long guard hairs; soft underfur	**VW**	standard daily care; clean every 2 years
silky guard hairs; woolly underfur	**VW**	avoid rain; annual cleaning
extremely long, soft full guard hairs; cushiony underfur	**VW**	avoid friction; annual cleaning
same	**VW**	same
same	**W**	same
same	**VW**	same
same	**W**	same
long, soft, thick guard hairs; cushiony underfur	**VW**	standard daily care; annual cleaning
long, soft guard hairs	**VW**	same
slightly coarse long, thick guard hairs; dense underfur	**VW**	same
short guard hairs; white belly fur; thick underfur	**W**	same

	Cost	Color	Durability
Marten			
American	$6,000–$25,000	wide range of colors from deep bluish brown and brown-black to pale yellow with orange tones	8–10 yrs.
Baum	$1,000–$25,000	taupey green brown; often dyed to resemble sable	8–10 yrs.
Stone	$7,000–$25,000	rosy beige or off-white underfur; taupe beige guard hairs	10 yrs. +
Muskrat	$750–$3,000	distinctive silver and black stripes on pale beige or silver fur	5–8 yrs.
Nutria	$1,800–$5,000	brown guard hairs; brown underfur; often dyed	10 yrs.
Opossum			
American	$1,000–$2,500	silver gray to gray black	8–10 yrs.
Rabbit	$500–$2,500	wide variety of colors; frequently dyed	3 yrs.
Raccoon	$1,800–$7,000	brown and gray underfur; silver and black highlights on guard hairs	10–15 yrs.
Skunk	*	distinctive black and white stripes	5–10 yrs.
Tanuki	$2,000–$8,500	red gold or blue gold with black-tipped guard hairs	10–15 yrs.

Texture	Warmth	Maintenance
long, slightly coarse hair; thick underfur	**W**	avoid soaking rains; standard daily care; clean every 2 years
long, soft, silky guard hairs	**VW**	same
longer guard hairs; cushiony underfur	**VW**	same
full thick guard hairs; dense underfur	**VW**	standard daily care; clean every 2 years; annual summer storage
plush, sleek guard hairs	**VW**	standard daily care; clean every 2 years
long flat hairs	**VW**	standard daily care; clean every 2 years; annual summer storage
soft, velvety	**W**	very fragile
thick, long guard hairs; very dense underfur	**VW**	standard daily care; clean every 2 years
long, glossy hairs	**W**	standard daily care; clean every 2 years; annual summer storage
thick, long guard hairs; very dense underfur	**VW**	standard daily care; clean every 2 years

LAMB

	Cost	Color	Durability
PROCESSED BROADTAIL	$1,500–$6,000	variety of colors; frequently dyed	5–8 yrs.
BROADTAIL	$5,000–over $20,000 +	variety of colors; frequently dyed	10 yrs. +
MONGOLIAN	$300–$2,000	off-white in natural state; frequently dyed	5–8 yrs.
PERSIAN	$1,000–$4,000	white gray to brown when natural; frequently dyed	10–15 yrs.

SHEARED FURS

		Cost	Color	Durability
BEAVER		$1,500–$8,000	usually dyed; rarely sold in natural state	10–12 yrs.
LAMB	*Mouton*	$500–$3,500	usually dyed in a wide range of colors	10 yrs.
	Shearling	$500–$3,500	creamy color in its natural state; frequently dyed	10 yrs.
MUSKRAT		$750–$2,500	distinctive silver and black stripes	10 yrs.
NUTRIA		$1,500–$5,000	medium brown in natural state; often blended to a deeper brown or dyed black	10 yrs.

Texture	Warmth	Maintenance
sheared to look like moiré pattern of broadtail	W	standard daily care; clean every 2 years; annual summer storage
flat moiré pattern	NW	avoid all rain; do not wear every day; annual summer storage
long, silky, curly hairs	W	standard daily care; annual summer storage
silky tight curls; soft leather	VW	standard daily care; annual summer storage
plush, velvety	VW	avoid rain; annual cleaning and summer storage
dense, soft	VW	water repellant; clean every 2 years; annual summer storage
curly, soft	VW	standard daily care; clean as necessary; annual summer storage
plush, velvety	VW	avoid rain; annual cleaning and summer storage
plush, velvety	VW	avoid rain; annual cleaning and summer storage

Buying Your Fur Coat

~

A fur is a luxury item, whether you spend one hundred thousand dollars on a sable coat or seven hundred dollars on a fox jacket. Seven hundred dollars is a lot of money to spend on something you're going to wear. If you're just looking for warmth, you can save yourself a lot of money and buy long underwear. Fur is for the pleasure and beauty. My philosophy is simple: You should love your coat; it has to make you feel ten feet tall.

Buying a fur is fraught with psychological booby traps—with fears about finding the right color and the right style at the right price—you don't need to add fears about your furrier's reliability on top of that. I firmly believe that whether you buy from a showroom like ours, a discount house, a small salon, or an elegant retail shop, you can find a furrier who is dependable, honest, and knowledgeable. You want to build a relationship with your furrier; then you can work together to find the type of fur and style that suits your expectations, needs, and lifestyle. In this section we will examine the types of fur stores available to you. I will share my insights about how to talk to a furrier and I'll offer you some guidelines for selecting the most flattering cut and fur.

4

Where to Buy a Fur

~

BUYING A FUR COAT is more challenging these days than it used to be because not only is the variety of furs greater but there are also so many more outlets to choose from. The fur business has boomed in the last decade. One-and-a-half billion dollars a year is spent on a wide variety of furs and styles that were disregarded a few years ago. Thousands of younger men and women are buying furs for themselves. For them, fur has become a necessary luxury.

To accommodate this new generation of customers, a carnival of new retail options has appeared on the scene. Once there were only specialty shops and posh fur salons in department stores. Today, there are many different types of fur outlets—mass-market retail furriers, elegant retail stores, designer boutiques, wholesale showrooms, discount furriers, caravan sales, and secondhand furriers.

Each one offers a different mix of the four most important attributes of a fur store—price, quality, service, and selection. Your job as an informed consumer is to find the source that offers the best mix of these qualities for you.

My personal recommendation is that you buy the best quality you can find at the lowest price, which means you may have to wait for preseason and postseason sales at retailers, wholesale showrooms, and fur salons. You have to be willing to defer gratification. But this may not be possible or desirable; after all, a fur sale doesn't necessarily occur on your birthday or anniversary.

So what should you do? To find the best coat at the best price:

1. Visit the many different furriers in your area.
2. Try on many different types and styles of fur.
3. Interview various furriers.
4. Get references and recommendations from friends.

If you have never owned a fur, your first step is simply to collect as much information as possible. Once you get the feel for fur, you can experience the delicious differences between a mink and a fox, a tanuki and a fisher, a sheared beaver and a lynx. Then you will be prepared to evaluate what looks best. Don't rush into a decision and don't let any salesperson pressure you. Enjoy trying on a wide variety of coats and visiting many furriers. To help you, I give you the pros and cons of the many types of fur shops. Before you start your tour, you'll know all the essentials about fur salons that offer pampered customer service as well as those that run self-service operations. You'll understand that there are those with enormous selections and those with a small, carefully chosen stock. Never forget that each one should offer basic customer services and guarantees, and wherever you buy a fur you should feel confident and comfortable with your purchase.

BASIC SERVICE REQUIREMENTS

You are entitled to require certain services when you buy a coat. You should be able to look to your furrier as someone to work with and depend on over the years. The basic services they should provide are:

~ Alterations to length of hem and sleeve.

~ Adjustment of closings.

~ Major alterations when required—such as taking in the size of the collar or lapel or adjusting the shoulder. Alterations are done before the coat is paid for in full. You always have approval privileges. Our policy is, "We own the coat until you approve it and pay for it." Until then you may choose another garment or get your deposit back.

~ Storage and cleaning facilities.

~ Appraisal for insurance.

Given these basic professional standards and customer services there are trade-offs you might want to make in order to get the coat you long for. The price and quality of any fur coat should be determined by the price of each skin used; the number of skins in the coat; the cost of labor; and the markup taken by the store. You may save on the cost but maintain the quality by juggling these variables. Perhaps you will choose a type of fur that is not premium priced or select a style that does not demand a large number of skins. Five years ago we made mink coats with approximately thirty-five skins; today, the popular fuller designs use more than fifty skins.

You may also save money by selecting a coat made overseas, where labor costs are significantly lower. This way, you may get the style or quality you want at a substantial saving. Only a few years ago, coats manufactured in the Far East were almost always made from poor quality skins and with lower quality workmanship than American or European coats. Today, you don't have to be wary of all imported coats. I used to be able to spot an imported coat a block away. These days, I have to see the label of some of them to be sure. My personal advice is that you can be confident of the value and quality of a coat if it is sold in a fine store or under the label of a top manufacturer, no matter where it is made. I must admit, we entrust our most costly skins only to the hands of our own craftsmen.

The last variable is in the markup or profit made by stores. You can find many shops that have high-volume sales and thereby take a smaller profit margin. You may give up some services and perhaps some quality.

Unfortunately, price alone is not a sure sign of savings or of quality. Dr. Russel R. Taylor, professor of marketing at the College of New Rochelle and author of books and articles on the fur industry, believes that one of the most disturbing trends in the fur industry is the use of markdown prices that don't reflect true discount. He points out that more and more furriers, even major retailers, tag their coats fifty percent off, when the coat never actually sold for twice the price. Therefore, he advises, it is your right to ask any furrier to show you proof that the coat was in fact sold at the higher price. This can be done by showing invoices and bills of sale. I suggest you beware of retailers who regularly advertise their furs at fifty to seventy-five percent off. We do occasionally mark a coat down that much postseason, when we want to move old merchandise or preseason to get off to a good start. But common sense tells us that nobody could do that all the time and stay in business. When reliable fur shops have occasional sales you can be relatively confident that you can find a bargain. But perpetual sales . . . I have my doubts about them and think you should, too.

FUR STORES

Fur stores range from small family-owned businesses that cater to a local clientele to huge mass-market operations that lease space in national department-store chains. They can be expensive or price worthy. What they all share in common is continuity, accountability, and a dedication to maintaining a good reputation. This does not mean that they are all equal. One small local furrier may have been serving their area for generations, while others may be new kids on the block. A department store may have well-trained, knowledgeable salespeople or students working their way through college. You need to assess the quality of each store.

Fur salons offer the average customer the easiest, most dependable way of shopping. They preselect the garments, can provide solid, ongoing service, and are interested in establishing a relationship with you.

ELEGANT DEPARTMENT STORES

Many stores such as Neiman-Marcus, Bullock's, and Bergdorf-Goodman are known for their fine fur departments. These retailers offer a blend of boutique luxury in standard retail operations. The result is that they staff their departments with experts and stock a variety of the best furs of many designers and manufacturers from across the country and around the world. You reap the benefits of their global buying.

Yale Kramer from Bullock's explains his store's policy: "We travel all over the world, to the Orient, to Copenhagen, to Frankfurt, and New York to find the latest styles and the best quality and value. We know what kind of style and quality our customer wants. In California and Texas, seventy-five percent of our furs are mink, about fifteen percent are fox, and ten percent are lynx and beaver. Seventy-five percent of the styles are current but not extreme. We tend to modify the most extreme high-fashion styles. Our long-standing relations with manufacturers lets us work with them to get the best designs for our customers."

When the customer enters a fine retail furrier, a lot of preselection and hard work have already been done for her.

She can assume that the experts have put together a line that is price worthy and of high quality. In an elegant retail store, the customer can be sure the quality and tastefulness of the furs will be consistent with the store's overall retail standards.

"We offer extensive customer service, as do all fine furriers. It is special, but it should be expected," Mr. Kramer says. Services at fine retail stores include:

~ Storage for the life of the garment at a nominal cost.
~ Cleaning and glazing.
~ Repairs. The stores do not make major repairs, but they work with fine furriers locally and supervise the work.
~ Remodeling. They will arrange for a furrier to meet any customer at the store to plan the remodeling of a coat, if desired.
~ Free care for any coat bought through them. If seams open after five years of wear, bring in the coat and they will have them resewn for free. Repairs of closing, buttons, pockets, hems, any such minor fix-ups, should be offered to any customer.

Advantages
1. The merchandise represents the expert judgment of the store. They have culled the best from many markets.
2. Service is of top quality.
3. Special benefits such as choice of linings, custom tailoring and alterations, and special orders can be arranged.

   4. Sales and in-store caravans offer you the chance to get all the retailer's advantages for reduced prices.

Disadvantages

   1. You are paying a premium for the name and label.

   2. You are limited by the taste and style of any one store. To find your look you must visit several and compare.

MASS-MARKET FUR STORES

There are now several national fur manufacturers and sellers that lease fur salons within department stores or have their own shops. Such chains are high volume, price conscious, and respond to fashion trends, offering their own versions of all the latest styles.

According to Fred Schwartz, president of The Fur Vault, a large fur-retailing business, "We are not really mass market . . . but a specific market. Traditionally the fur business catered to ten percent of the population. We have expanded the market to include thirty percent. It's still not mass, just a broader range than before."

But whatever you call these shops, they offer many different varieties of furs at various prices and have opened up a dazzling array of possibilities for the consumer: average price, high quality; high price, top quality; and low price, lesser quality coats are all sold under one roof. To know if it is the right store for your needs you must depend heavily on:

   ~ The local reputation of the furrier. The only way to find out is to ask people who have bought their coats there.

~ The knowledge of the sales staff. They will try to give you the best coat for your dollar if you know how to talk to them. (Chapter Five explains how to talk to a furrier.) "Any true furrier understands that he can't rush a customer. The salespeople want to build a relationship with you more than they want to sell you a coat," stresses Mr. Schwartz.

~ Your ability to read the craftsmanship of a fur.

Advantages

1. A national reputation backs up their merchandise.
2. They have combed the fur market. They have seen everything that's available. They have searched for quality and price. And then they have used their judgment and expertise to cull what they consider best. (Every retail outlet, at any level, offers this advantage; however, the judgment about what is best for their customers differs according to the needs of their particular clientele.)
3. Volume in particular styles or furs allows for significant price breaks. Large turnover (five times a year at Fred Schwartz's various outlets) assures you of a wide selection of coats.
4. They provide service and repairs. Full service is available, from minor alterations and repairs to special orders and major remodeling.
5. Advertised specials offer a chance to get the fur you want at a low price.

Disadvantages

1. Very top quality skins and furs are not available.
2. The large volume makes a relationship with a sales-

person less personal than in a smaller operation. But do not allow any furrier to treat you cavalierly.

3. You cannot be sure that every fur in the store is of the same quality. You must be able to evaluate quality on your own.

4. There is always a chance of bumping into other people who have on the same fur that you are wearing.

SMALL SALONS

The furrier who has run a local shop for a generation can offer many people dependability and personal service. Smaller fur retailers comb the New York fur market for the best selections, but their stock is limited. The coats they carry tend to reflect the tastes of your particular locality, and may be just what you want. Prices will be higher than in some retail outlets because volume is low. Word-of-mouth recommendations from their customers are always a good guide to your trust in their service.

Some small salons may not be set up to deal with repairs, particularly if fur needs to be replaced in a worn-out section of your coat. These salons can, if they know their business, contact the same top-quality matchers as any larger retailer and send the work out to the finest craftsmen in the country. However, some may be equipped to do repair work or even custom make a coat.

"I would not hesitate to go to a small local furrier," says Sandra Crow, a former resident buyer at Joseph Modell. "Most have operated as family businesses for two to three generations. They are very savvy." If you want to make sure they have access to the New York markets and contacts with the best manufacturers, she suggests you ask if they use a resident fur buyer. Almost all of them will, and if they don't, it may indicate a lack of real knowledge or of connections to the fur market.

Ask friends about their experiences with repairs and service. Query the furrier to find out how such situations are handled. The furrier should provide the basic services outlined at the beginning of this chapter. Your personal relationship with the furrier is vital in such an environment.

Advantages

1. Years of local service assure you of the salon's good reputation.
2. A small shop can provide the most intimate of customer services.
3. Long-term relationships with clients let local furriers shop with you in mind. When they go to the market to buy coats, they can look for just what you want.

Disadvantages

1. Low volume may mean smaller selection and variety.
2. Prices may be higher than at other retailers.

MANUFACTURERS' SHOWROOMS

Many manufacturers like Goldin-Feldman in the fur district in New York, who produce the garments that the stores sell, have opened their showrooms to customers. These days, if you want a designer label you often buy it directly from the manufacturer. The showrooms range from elegant salons that pamper individual customers and buyers from stores to slightly ramshackle storefronts with factories and workrooms behind them. Each showroom has its particular brands, styles, and models of coats. You can find out who these individual manufacturers are by checking advertisements in fashion magazines for the names of the manufacturers of different designer labels, or by word of mouth.

Manufacturers have been obliged to open their doors to the public because a large percentage of the retail department stores, especially in New York City, now lease their fur departments to fur companies who prefer to trade under the store name rather than their own. This makes it impossible for a manufacturer to sell to these department stores or for consumers in New York to find one of these coats unless they go to a showroom. A few stores like Bergdorf-Goodman and Neiman-Marcus still run their own fine fur departments, but it is becoming more and more unusual.

While this has been a hardship for the manufacturers, cutting the number of New York–based firms from two thousand to six hundred in recent years, it gives the consumer a great opportunity to buy the designer and nondesigner coats at a considerable savings. Our showroom is geared to make the consumer as comfortable as possible and offers a full range of professional services. After all, you are buying the coat where it was made. If there are any alterations to be done, they are made by the same craftsmen who created the coat in the first place. And many manufacturers in the fur district have been in business for several generations. This assures you of a commitment to quality and a continuity of reputation that is unquestionable. Despite the fact that showrooms have customers from all over the country—in fact, from around the world—they are able to give you the personal attention and service you need. Repairs, alterations, and restylings can all be done, and we can get a coat to you in one day! So if you like the idea of combing the New York market, showrooms offer these advantages and disadvantages.

Manufacturers' Designer Labels Because manufacturers produce designer label coats, I am asked about them all the time. Consumers wonder what a designer label really means and if they pay a premium for the name. Yves St. Laurent, Giancarlo Ripa, Hanae Mori, Karl Lagerfeld, Geoffrey Beene and Chloé have all designed furs for us. When we contract with a designer to create a line of furs it is the beginning of a collaborative effort that depends on the designer's imagination and fashion sense and on the skills of our master craftsmen. A designer will send us sketches from which we select the ones we want to have made up into rough canvas coats to fit on our models. We then alter them to accommodate the design requirements of fur.

Designer furs tend to be the highest styled coats in any season and they open up a world of possibilities to the American consumer. One of the things that happens is that, just like in the clothing business, less expensive knockoffs are made of the designer styles. Over and over our designs have been copied by other furriers and their pizzazz gets lost in the translation. Our response has been to develop our own lines of knockoffs, using the same fine designs and manufacturing standards as the originals but making them using less costly labor and in varieties of furs that are less expensive.

I think that it is important when you try on designer furs to keep your sense of what looks best on you. Just as you accept or reject the look of designer clothes, so you can judge designer furs. My advice is, unless you have money to burn, stay away from styles, types of furs, and designs that are not durable, will date quickly, or are too outrageous to be worn most places. When you do find a designer coat that suits your style you get fine quality and don't necessarily have to pay a premium. They go on sale, too, and are available at department store caravans, in pre- and post-season sales, and through manufacturers' showrooms, like ours.

Advantages
1. The prices are usually good.
2. The craftspeople who make the coats are right there. They can assure you of a perfect fit and answer all your questions.
3. Quality is assured but does vary, just as the quality of different designer coats varies.
4. A custom-designed coat can be made from a pattern cut just for you, and you can select the pelts.

Disadvantages
1. You may have to travel a great distance to visit the showrooms. If you are from out of town, you will have to build a long-distance relationship with the furrier.
2. You will see only the styles and types of furs that the

showroom specializes in. For variety, you will have to go to many different locations.

3. There are manufacturers who are less reputable than others. Without knowing their local reputation, you may not know when you have met one of the lower-quality manufacturers. Some "showrooms" are really just retailers exploiting the fur district's reputation for good prices.

SPECIALTY STORES WITH FUR DEPARTMENTS

More recently women's specialty stores have begun to add fur departments. They usually sell less expensive fur coats and jackets to their customers who buy their ready-to-wear. They are conveniently located in hometowns and malls and are already familiar with the needs and desires of their customers. They are helpful in that they offer layaway plans and take credit cards. It is a nonintimidating way for the "first fur" customer to shop. Often the specialty stores are part of a chain, which gives them the power to buy in quantity and therefore sell at a good price. They stock furs like other garments, buying a few styles across the board in selected sizes and colors.

Advantages

1. Familiar surroundings for the customer.
2. Can delay payment through layaway and charge plans.
3. They are conveniently located and know their customers well.
4. Offer a large selection of sizes and colors.

Disadvantages
1. They have little ability to do alterations and customer styling.
2. They usually have a limited choice of more commercial styles.
3. They usually don't offer storage.

THE DISCOUNT OPTION

For the woman who knows what she wants or who simply wants to browse undisturbed, the discount option offers an inexpensive alternative to higher-priced retail stores or fur salons. There are many types of discounts available—some more risky than others; therefore, in general, I recommend that the consumer makes sure she knows the name, location, and phone number of the corporate office that runs the sale.

Understand the repair, refund, and replacement policy. In the event that you damage your coat, will they make repairs? For a fee? If your coat is defective and it is their fault, will they stand behind it? Also make sure the tag on each coat identifies the country of origin of the skins, where the coat was made, and whether the fur is natural or processed, or color enhanced.

CARAVAN SALES

One discount option is caravan sales, which are traveling, instant discount stores set up in hotels, auditoriums, or retail shops. They offer hundreds or thousands of furs from many sources for a limited time. You will often see announcements for them in local papers. Fall is the prime season.

Department Store Caravans   Caravans vary. Some caravans are run by department stores. Major retailers from large cities may travel to smaller cities to sell furs. For these sales they offer a combination of their regular line of furs, sale items that may be left over from last year's inventory, manufacturers' specials and some pieces that are particularly inexpensive, and imported versions of popular styles.

Yale Kramer, the fur merchandise manager for Bullock's and Sanger Harris department stores, explains their caravan policy: "Once a year we run in-store caravan sales. We bring in furs from the markets and add them to our regular collections. We add both more expensive furs that can be sold at our advantageous price and less expensive imports that appeal to bargain hunters. The caravan travels from store to store. It offers tremendous savings for a few days."

Sandra Crow works with large and small retail furriers, acting as purchasing agent in the New York fur market. "For such caravans," she explains, "we might help a store augment its regular line with special furs, so the consumer has a very wide selection of furs and prices to choose from."

Such caravans, run by high-quality retailers, are an interesting option. To get the coat you want at the considerable savings these caravans offer, you have to be willing to wait for the opportunity provided by these once- or twice-a-year sales. If you can wait, you will be getting a bargain *and* reliability. Retailers are available to work with you over the years on repairs and maintenance problems on these sale coats, just as they are on their full-priced products.

Manufacturers' Caravans   Well-known manufacturers and designers also conduct caravan sales. Like department stores, they offer a mixture of top-line merchandise and low-cost sale specials. These events are widely advertised in local papers. Be on the lookout for them around Christmastime and during March and August.

Manufacturers' caravans do not always offer a full range of customer service. "Women with figure problems or special needs should always go to very reputable furriers," advises Sandra Crow.

If you are interested in a coat that requires only moderate alterations, then you can expect such needs to be met at top-quality caravan fur sales. If you find a caravan that skimps on basic services, move on!

Fur-Broker Caravans   These caravans are somewhat more risky. They are arranged by brokers who transport a high volume of goods all over the country and hold sales in hotels and auditoriums. They are not affiliated with any store, manufacturer, or designer. You cannot be sure, by the name, that you are dealing with a reputable and fair furrier. When their advertisements appear in local papers, read the copy carefully. If they do not identify designers or manufacturers or country of origin, approach the merchandise with caution.

Larry Cowit, who deals in used furs and has supplied furs to various caravan and discount dealers over the years, cautions: "The prices are not always a real savings. Either they are just as high as the stores or the quality is lower, so you are getting less for less money."

When it comes to buying at caravans, the burden of making the right decision rests on you. You must be able to judge the furs, to know the value, and to accept the disadvantages as well as the advantages.

Advantages
1. Prices can be very low, even on quality items.
2. The huge number of coats available allows you to try on a wide range of furs in many styles.
3. The self-service atmosphere makes a caravan a good place to start your fur education. You can compare and browse.
4. You have a chance to buy a fur locally if your town doesn't offer a selection of retail stores.

Disadvantages
1. The advice and expertise of a personal furrier will not always be available.
2. Except for retail caravans, you cannot expect to build a personal relationship with a furrier that will last over time.
3. There is no local store or office to contact if there is a problem with the coat.
4. The quality of the furs offered may vary widely. You must be able to judge them.
5. Discount prices may not be any lower than standard or sale retail prices.

PERMANENT DISCOUNT STORES
There are permanent discount furriers who offer dramatic savings on a continuing basis. They may be affiliated

with a manufacturer, sell their own furs and an assortment of imports, or scour the fur market for close-outs that can be bought and resold at very substantial savings. Some of these stores have established local reputations and offer the security of being there if you have a complaint or a question. If you choose to buy from such a store, make sure they stand behind their merchandise and have them outline their quality assurance. I remember one incident in New York when a dissatisfied customer of a discount store had to resort to picketing the shop to try and get compensation for flaws in a coat she had purchased. Try to save your shoe leather by carefully evaluating discount stores.

Advantages
1. The high volume and large selection result in a wide choice of furs under one roof.
2. Discount prices may make a more expensive fur a reality for you.
3. The permanent location reduces the risks associated with temporary caravan sales.

Disadvantages
1. You must depend on your ability to evaluate the quality of each individual fur, since there is a wide variety offered.
2. You do not get the personal service offered in a smaller store.
3. Styles tend to be standard or classic, not high fashion.
4. In some instances, discounts are more illusion than reality, since quality is lowered as price comes down.

SECONDHAND FURRIERS

Secondhand furs are a good alternative for the price-conscious consumer. They offer furs at about one-third the original price, and when the furriers are reputable, you have a choice of fine-quality labels. Used furs do not have to be abused furs.

A low-priced used mink, for example, made by an excellent furrier, can still be in great shape after eight to ten years of wear.

As with any fur, use the basic guidelines when shopping. Check the suppleness of the skins, the luster of the hair, the quality of the original workmanship. There are some additional precautions you should take with used furs as well:

1. Always check the key wear spots: the top of each shoulder where purse straps can rub off the fur, sleeve edges, pocket openings, the "sit spot" on the back of the coat, buttonholes or loops, and collars.

2. Check beneath the lining. Ask the shop to open up the lining if it is sewn shut. Are the seams between pelts dried or frayed? Can they be repaired, or is the skin so dry they will continue to reopen? Has the fur been dyed? If the skin is dark it probably has been dyed, and this will shorten the life of the fur.

3. Check the label. It should specify country of origin, type of fur, and whether it is natural or dyed. If it doesn't state these things, ask why.

4. If you are serious about getting a fine used fur, don't pay cash and carry because you will not have a chance

to supervise the repair work as it is being done. You
will be buying the fur "as is."

The best used-fur shops display their coats unrepaired.
You get to see what it is that you are buying, problems and
all. They will take a deposit from you and make the repairs
and alterations you desire. If you are happy with the coat,
then you pay the balance. If the coat does not measure up to
the promised repairs, they should refund your money.
Avoid resale shops that don't work like this.

Furthermore, the price agreed on should be inclusive—
no add-ons, no hidden charges. Alterations should be free
and storage included. A resale furrier should offer the
dependability of a retail shop.

According to Michael Kosoff, the owner of the Ritz
Thrift Shop in New York City, "A customer must be happy
with the fur. We always give refunds, even after full purchase is made, if the coat doesn't measure up." The Ritz
also will hold the coat while you make time payments,
which makes it even more affordable.

If you find a good source for used furs, it is a way to
make your dream come true. If you are comfortable with
the idea of a secondhand fur, it can be a good investment.

Advantages

1. Fine furs, beyond your budget when new, are often
   affordable when used.
2. Classic styling and workmanship on older furs make
   them special.

Disadvantages

1. A used fur will obviously not have the wearing life of a new one. If price is a major consideration, this is a viable compromise.
2. Many used-fur shops operate on a cash-and-carry basis, which can be risky.
3. Used coats that have been refurbished before you see them can have hidden problems.

By the time you are ready to decide which furrier offers you the best mix of service, selection, quality, and price, you may have visited many locations or you might have been lucky enough to have had a referral to the perfect shop. In either case, as you try on coats, talk to sales personnel and ask questions; you will begin to know what suits you. In the following chapter, advice on evaluating a furrier and talking to him or her will hone your skills even more.

5

How to Talk to a Furrier

~

A GOOD FURRIER not only has fine-quality merchandise but has the instincts of a mind reader and the sympatico of a friend. You want to establish a relationship so that you can be confident in your furrier's advice and assurances of quality and can depend on his or her help in finding the coat that is perfectly suited to your look and lifestyle. You also want a furrier who will tell you when a coat is *not* for you.

Recently a very pretty woman with a small, delicate face and a full head of curly hair was torn between two coats in our showroom, one with a large notched lapel and one with a trim mandarin collar. As she tried on one coat and then the other, it became clear to me that the full collar overwhelmed her face. The smaller collar, however, complemented her face and was a beautiful accent to her hair. Once she took her eyes off the coats and looked at her own face, she could see what I meant. Any salesperson who says you look equally good in every item you put on is not being honest. My attitude is that if I don't sell a particular coat to one customer, there will be another one who will look great in it. A coat may be on the rack for a while—it just may not have worked for the women who have tried it on—and then one day someone tries it on and it's perfect!

Not all fur shops, however, will have the type of service or merchandise that suits you, and even in those that do, you want to be an active, alert buyer. You want to make good, solid decisions based on informed opinions and your well-placed trust in the furrier you have chosen to work with. The only way to forge this mutually beneficial relationship is to approach each shop with an inquisitive, open mind and a shrewd eye. From the first minute you walk into a salon you are getting valuable information about the quality and style of the operation.

FIRST IMPRESSIONS

When you walk into a fur shop you want to watch the other customers talking with the salespeople, sense their style and taste, feel the tempo of the store. Tune into what you see, feel, and hear. Remember, you aren't there to buy the chandelier, so don't be overimpressed by the decor. On the other hand, a tasteful, well-lit showroom does make the furs look more beautiful and you may feel more comfortable if you like the environment.

Once you have taken in your first impression of the

business itself you want to meet and evaluate the salespeople. A furrier's task is to help you find what you are looking for, even if you aren't sure of exactly what that is. If you walk in the door and a salesman says, "I have a great ranch mink for you," he's not taking the time to find out about you. He is trying to sell any coat, not match one to you. If you get that feeling proceed with caution.

Salespeople should not immediately categorize you, either. But you do want to feel that they see you and can direct your shopping by suggesting that you try on coats that will complement your look and style. What I try to do is to decide if a person is classic or high-fashion in overall appearance, and then if they favor tailored or softer styled clothes. I try to be sensitive to how a customer wants to look. It can be helpful for the furrier, and for the customer, if she comes dressed in an appropriate style. For example, if you are going to be wearing your coat over business suits, you will be able to judge its fit and look better if that's what you wear when you go shopping. You may not be able to wear a ballgown for trying on formal furs, but bringing a change of shoes may help.

You want to gather as much information about the shop and its sales approach as you can in those first few minutes, so you can communicate what your needs and opinions are, as well. Once you have begun trying on various coats, share your reactions with the furrier. Don't ever be ashamed to be a novice, and don't feel it means you can't have definite opinions about the color, cut, or style of a fur that appeals to you. You may feel vague about your knowledge, but speak up anyway. Tell the salesperson, "I usually like big shoulders," or "I'm crazy about light-colored furs," or "I never think I look good in wide or full coats." Any opinion will help him respond to your needs. What I find most difficult is when a customer says, "I'll know it when I see it." The choices available are so varied that it's hard to know where to start.

So my suggestion is, if you really don't know how to express what you're looking for, at least share these three points of information: if this is your first or only fur; if you want an everyday fur or one for formal or occasional wear; and your general price range (although, as I'll explain later, don't be too specific too early).

Once you've gotten through this much of a conversation with the furrier you will be well on your way to knowing if this is the place for you. There is a lot going on but it should be fun to find out about the coats they have and their particular methods of doing business. To help you, I've come up with eight very important questions that I think you should discuss with every furrier.

WHAT KIND OF QUALITY ASSURANCE DO YOU OFFER?

If you spill flaming cherries jubilee on your coat, you can't expect your furrier to replace it with a new one; if you wear a heavy shoulder bag on your mink every day for years, it's not the furrier's fault that the hairs become matted or broken. However, if you've taken good care of a coat and it doesn't meet reasonable expectations he should be willing to make minor repairs (or major, in some circumstances) at minimal or no cost to you. A good furrier is dedicated to preserving his reputation and can express his policy without hesitation. At Goldin-Feldman we guarantee that we have in no way misrepresented the coat either verbally or on the tag; we give a very detailed written insurance appraisal, and we will do alterations and reasonable repairs at no charge within the first year. After that, minor repairs are free, others are made at cost. When we sell a coat we expect you to get years of pleasure from it and don't want you to feel abandoned.

DO YOU PROVIDE STORAGE?

Every good furrier offers storage, usually at a nominal fee. This means the company will be there for you; they'll see the coat again and can help maintain it. Some caravan and discount shops may not provide this service, but you should not hesitate to take your coat to any reputable furrier, even if you did not purchase it from him. Storage is part of their business and they will welcome your patronage.

While a coat is being stored for the summer it can be cleaned and glazed (see maintenance tips in Chapter Seven). This too should be a standard option offered at a nominal price. It is worth it, for cleaning and reglazing, like summer storage, will prolong the life of the coat.

DO YOU PROVIDE FREE ALTERATIONS?

Many fine furs, even the perfect one for you, may need some alterations before it is ready for you to wear it. Most furriers offer this as part of the price of the coat. Our policy is to make sure the coat fits as if it had been custom made for the buyer at no additional charge.

The standard free alterations are the length of the sleeves, the length of the garment, and the placement of closings and monogramming.

Additional alterations, such as adjusting the width of the sleeve, the depth of the armhole, and the fit of the shoulder and back of the coat may not be included by all furriers. These alterations can be intricate and labor intensive.

MAY I LEAVE A DEPOSIT BEFORE ALTERATIONS AND PAY IN FULL ON APPROVAL?

If you buy a coat that needs alterations, either minor or major, you should be able to approve these changes before you pay for the coat. If you don't approve them, they should be done to your satisfaction or your deposit should be refunded. The amount of the deposit itself may vary but it should only be a fraction of the price of the coat.

DO I HAVE A CHOICE OF LININGS?

Most furs come with silk or silk-blend linings already sewn in, but in some instances you may choose one. If you do I recommend pure silk, even though it does not wear as well as blends, because it is lighter and drapes well. The color of a lining should complement the fur color and the pattern should be basic enough that it won't clash with patterned dresses that you may wear.

WHAT IS YOUR POLICY ON MINOR REPAIRS?

Minor repairs include resewing on buttons, repairing linings and pockets, and resewing the seams of the skins. Yale Kramer of Bullock's and Sanger Harris explained that minor repairs are done free for the life of the fur by many high-quality furriers. You may not get such pampering from everyone, and it may be a trade-off that you are willing to make to get the coat you want at a price you can afford.

DO YOU PERFORM MAJOR REPAIRS?

With time, any fur will begin to show wear at the elbows, buttonholes, cuffs, front edges, hemline, pocket edges, or along the sides of the collar. Some of these repairs are possible and some are just not worth doing. When considering a major repair the most important factor is, will you want to wear the coat once they are done? Major repairs can be very expensive and you don't want to spend money on them if you're not going to get the results you want. Our policy is that we won't do repairs unless they will be invisible when they are completed. Since we have the craftsmen and facilities to do these major jobs, we are able to take on expensive renovations of out-of-style or worn furs. Many fur shops do not have an in-house staff who can do such jobs, but they should have a liaison with a reliable furrier so that your coat can be sent out with confidence for repairs. Ask for (and get) exact charges before repairs are done. Ask about how the repair will be handled. Anyone who can't answer those questions is not for you. If you ever need repair work on your coat you want the best. Repair work is like cosmetic surgery. . . you can't return it.

WHAT IS YOUR PRICE RANGE?

By finding out the high and low prices of a salon's minks or whatever fur you are looking at, you can tell if you will be able to find what you want in your price range without having to say exactly what you want to spend. Furthermore, it is helpful to look at various priced examples of each fur in order to train your eyes and hands to sense the differences in quality. Only you can know what makes you happy and what will seem price worthy. But I know that if you love your coat, you will quickly forget how much you paid for it, and if you don't love it, you will never forget the cost.

The most important aspect of discussing prices with your furrier is to remember that he is supposed to be working *with* you. You may not want to reveal exactly what your budget is immediately but don't try to impress the furrier with how much money you can spend. Start low—you can always go up. If a furrier understands that you really have to stick to a budget, he or she may try to help you out by giving you a price break on a fur. It does happen. Don't be embarrassed to say that something is out of your price range. You are the customer—and even if all you have is twenty-five hundred dollars, that's a lot to spend on something you wear.

I really want to find a coat for each customer. When the budget is limited I'll show coats that I'm able to discount. I'll search until I find a coat that fits a customer's price range and taste. I once had a young woman in the showroom who said very frankly that she had two thousand dollars to spend. She really wanted a fur but knew that her options might be limited. I enjoy working with such a customer because I know when we find the right coat, it is a real dream come true. As a result, I went into our fur vault and found a raccoon coat that I was able to sell at a price that she could afford. It looked marvelous on her and since then she and her friends have returned again and again. There is a real satisfaction in making this kind of sale.

Once you have discussed these important points with the furrier and have sampled their selection of furs and styles, you will know if it's time to try another shop or if this may be the source for you. You may have gotten a great recommendation or simply been fortunate and have found a furrier you can work with at the very first store you visited. But if that's not the case, enjoy the exploration and don't settle for less than what makes you really happy. As you shop around remember these basic guidelines for good communication with your furrier:

Rule 1. Always tell the furrier how frequently and in what situations you will be wearing the fur. This lets him find the best variety of fur for you.

Rule 2. Tell the furrier what you like and don't like about each coat you try on. Be as specific as possible.

Rule 3. Ask the furrier what he or she thinks about the quality of the coat and how it looks on you.

Rule 4. Don't let any furrier pressure you. You should feel free to leave, come back, try on coats over and over. But remember, if you haven't fallen in love with a coat by the third date, get another date.

Rule 5. Let your sense be your final guide. Choose a furrier and a fur that make you happy.

A furrier should offer you the best service and quality

you can afford. As you shop around and try on different furs, you will find the store that has the styles you love. If the furrier can offer you the customer service and dependability you are looking for, you have found the right source.

6

Choosing Your Fur Coat

~

WHEN IT COMES TIME to work with your furrier to find the right style coat for your physique and lifestyle, you have a lot of choices. I think you can always expect to find a fur style that flatters your best features, enhances your beauty, and affects how you feel about yourself. When you put on the coat that has the right color fur and the right cut, it should make you glow just as if you'd just applied blush. To find a coat that has that effect, you want to learn how to look objectively, not just at the coat itself but at your face and form.

Over and over, a woman will come into the showroom and say, "My friend bought a silver fox and she looks great. I want one just like it." She neglects to mention that her friend is a lanky, raven-haired, ivory-skinned beauty, while she is a full-figured honey blonde. For her to find a coat that she will love, not just at the moment she sees it on the hanger, but season after season as she wears it, she needs to take a clear-eyed look at her own qualities and to know that it's not her fault if a particular coat doesn't look good on her. There are women who bestow more power on a fur than is appropriate. A fur can light up her face and flatter her figure, but it can't make her a new person. As my father sometimes says to a customer who complains that a coat makes her look too fat, "This is a fur salon, not a gymnasium, and you're going to leave here weighing the same as when you came in." A sense of humor will help you keep things in perspective as you evaluate how the coats look on you.

There are women who have prejudices against certain furs before they even try them on. Some feel that mink is only for older women, which is a completely outdated idea. Today, minks are highly styled and are worn on college campuses and by women who are homemakers and professionals. The choice of colors and variety of cuts and styles are as diverse as the imaginations of the world's best designers. There are also prejudices against long-haired furs. Some women feel these furs are too flashy. Fox, tanuki, raccoon, fisher, and beaver are all available in styles that make them appropriate for urban, suburban, and exurban lifestyles.

Unrealistic expectations, a poor self-image, and misconceptions about how you look or what you can wear can keep you from being able to see the best coat for you when you put it on. That's why it is important to find a furrier who will talk to you, point out your best features—not just the coat's—and help you to gain a clear picture of the right choices.

STYLING CHOICES

Finding the best style for you is important because the coat is a considerable investment and will be with you for a long time. There are many styling options available and each one has its own impact. A fur can become traditional or fashion-forward with a change of collar or the rise and fall of the shoulder pads. There are a lot of different choices when it comes to selecting the style of collar, shoulders, and sleeves you want. Although there are standard fashion rules that have been trotted out for decades—that, say, short women should never do this, or tall women always have to do that—I don't think they necessarily apply. To me, proportion is more important than any hard-and-fast rule. I've found the size of a woman's face can have as much to do with the kinds of fur and styling that look best on her as how tall, short, thin, or heavy she is. A petite woman with an open, strong face can carry off a long-haired lynx better than a small-faced, delicately featured tall woman can. A woman's inner image when combined with her physical proportions can make or break a coat.

So, the first thing you should look at when you put on a coat is the basic styling and its immediate impact. Don't get hung up on details, just slip on the coat. Does it make you smile? If it does, then you want to focus on the particulars of the style to fine tune your selection. Let's take it from the top.

THE COLLAR

The size, shape, and color of the collar are the frame for your face, and perhaps the most important style choices you will make. There are five options. The notched collar is the men's suit-styled version with a lapel. The collar and lapel can be narrow, medium, or wide. The notch, or dividing point between collar and lapel, can be set high, medium, or low. Low notched collars provide a deep, dramatic V. The high notched collars close securely at the neck and are very warm and may be converted into a mandarin when they are turned up. The shawl collar, with its softer, fuller lines, has a tailored yet romantic look that suits many women; it is an unnotched lapel and can be made in various widths. The mandarin, or oriental stand-up collar, is another type and for many women its classic, timeless style is best; the wing collar is an oversized mandarin that can be worn straight up or folded down. It comes in various proportions. The tuxedo collar has an open, full facing that extends to the hemline. There are also all kinds of styles that can be created by designers—from V-neck to asymmetrical.

Experiment with all the different collar styles to see what is most flattering for you. As you do this you will notice that the finishing details on each collar are very important. The collar and lapels on a fine mink have a soft fullness yet contain enough French lamb's wool and a very moldable metal stay so that you can adjust the collar and it will stay where you put it.

In long-haired furs, a stiffener called lamb tack and tape wire are used to give body and shape to the collar and lapel area. While these are somewhat stiffer than lamb's wool, it should not be obvious that they are in there doing their job.

THE SHOULDERS

The fit of the shoulders affects the drape of the entire garment and can determine the look of the coat. A full, thick, long-haired fur looks overwhelming if the shoulders are too big. The same coat with perfectly tailored shoulders appears trimmer and more flattering. A coat feels heavier if it falls back and doesn't hug the contour of the back of the neck. When adjusting the fit of a coat the back of the neck is often tightened to get the shoulders to sit correctly. It changes the look, feel, and fall of the coat.

There are several different tailoring techniques: the classic, the square, the dropped, the set-in, the raglan, the saddle, and the yoke. Each style can be adapted to the fashions of the time; they are all fine ways of constructing a beautiful fur coat.

Also, each coat style and each woman require a different amount of shoulder padding. For some customers we pile up three pads on each shoulder; for others we take the stuffing out of one thin pad to make it as flat as possible. I can't tell you how often I hear one customer say, "I don't want to look like a football player," and then five minutes later I hear another say, "I want really big shoulders." You need to try and see what works best with the lines of the coat you are wearing and with the size of your face, fall of your hair, length of your neck, and your body shape.

THE DRAPE OF THE COAT

If the shoulders are well-tailored and suit your taste and style, then you want to look at the general drape of the coat. There are basically five variations: the fitted (single- or double-breasted); the A-line; the demi-fit, which is tailored in the front and flared in the back; the full flared; and the straight line—either slim or boxy.

When you check the drape of a coat make sure that is lies evenly and smoothly and that the front hangs together even when unbuttoned. We make our coats with a two-inch facing of fur inside the front closing. Some coats have the lining right up to the front edge. This is an easy way to skimp on skin count.

The key to making any of these lines look good on you is to keep the proportions balanced. A small woman can wear a big flared coat if the coat is precisely tailored and the collar and sleeves are not overwhelming. Susan Lucci, who plays Erica Kane on "All My Children," wears all kinds of lush, full foxes, lynx, and other long-haired furs that we make for the show. And she is stunning in them, even though she is petite. The trick? The right proportion.

THE HEMLINE

The overall length of a coat changes with the seasons' styles, but I believe that it should be long enough to wear over day or evening clothes without being stepped on when you go up or down stairs. An average coat is made to be about nine inches off the floor in front, a half inch longer on the sides, and an inch longer in the back when you are wearing flats. Short women may find that a half inch shorter than this all around is better. Tall women may need up to two inches more length. But these are just guidelines, not rules. Let your own taste and comfort be your guide.

No matter what length a coat is, the most flattering and best-tailored hemlines end in a soft, even scalloping across the bottom. You only need a half-inch hem to get this effect. In mink two inches is the maximum depth for a hem—any wider and it becomes bulky and doesn't hang properly. Long-haired furs do not have any hem turned under.

THE SLEEVES

Sleeves are a wonderfully flexible part of a coat's style, for they can be as neat and trim or as big and eye catching as you like. These days, on many coats the sleeve fur is positioned in horizontal bands or spirals that contrast with the fall of the fur on the coat body. Overall, sleeves have gotten fuller because women now wear their winter coats over blazers, suits, and heavy sweaters. Years ago, women wore only dresses under their coats, but as they have entered the business world and as clothing styles have become more diverse, their furs must now function as true overcoats. The style choices in sleeves are: kimono, with its flared, cuffless end; raglan, which falls from the deep raglan shoulder; and the classic straight sleeve from a set-in shoulder. The construction can be altered by changing the depth of the arm hole and width of the sleeve. Your choice should be influenced by the length of your arms and the width of your body.

THE CUFFS

The way a sleeve ends has a great deal of impact on the general styling impression of a coat. Luckily, however, it is something you can change your mind about, since they are often easy to alter. Your basic choices are: full turned-back or stationary rolled-back cuffs; small banded cuffs; tab cuffs; elasticized sleeve ends; and straight hems. In a wide sleeve opening you may want to put in a wind guard to keep out the cold, and a too narrow opening may make it hard to pull the coat on over jewelry and gloves.

If you are trying to find some styling detail to economize on, remember this: It takes two extra skins to put full cuffs on a mink coat. That can increase the price by several hundred dollars.

LININGS

There are various types of linings used in fur coats. Silk organza is sewn into minks and other well-made, short-haired furs, from the hemline to the pockets. This lies directly against the leather to help the coat wear better and keep it from bagging. Over this, top-of-the-line minks have a preliminary lining made of silesia, which fits snugly into the garment and protects the skin. The final, outer lining, made of silk or a silk-synthetic blend, can sometimes be customized in the color and pattern you select. When it is done to order, it is like having a silk dress handmade, and it can take a finisher up to five hours to make it. I favor pure silk lining because although it is not as sturdy as blends, it doesn't alter the drape or increase the weight of the coat.

The ideal way to finish a short-haired coat is a French hem, which means that the hem is not attached to the coat but hangs separately and is tethered by taut strands of thread.

Long-haired furs tend to have hems attached to the body of the coat, as do jackets. These hems should be invisible, hand-sewn, and pucker-free. A hem that is machine-sewn is an indication of an overall lower standard of craftsmanship.

CLOSINGS

Closings should be used but not seen. We place a small button and a flat elastic band along the collar edge to secure the top of the lapel. Below that, by the waist, we put two American hooks. These are attached to the surface of the coat, unlike European hooks, which are larger and require that a hole be made in the fur fabric. On fuller coats to help you batten down the hatches against the cold winter winds a loop and double-string tie are added inside on the left and right side of the coat. Most closings are as inconspicuous as possible but you may want buttons for a special fashion look. Just remember that they do have some disadvantages: After several seasons the fur around them can become matted down or worn; the buttonholes themselves can snag and wear the fur.

MONOGRAMMING

Monogramming is a personal touch that is offered by almost all fur salons. It is not just a little extra that appeals to your vanity; it is important to have it done so that your coat is clearly recognizable. I mention monogramming here, not because it is a sign of quality in a coat, but because many people take as long to choose their monogram as they do to buy their coat. For some, it is an agonizing decision; for others, a matter of finding the right clever phrase. One customer had "With Love, from Ted" put in her coat. It was only fair, she said, since her husband was paying for it, even if he didn't know about it yet. In another instance, a famous singer used the title of her best-selling song, and a loving husband had "You deserve it!" put on a coat that was a gift. You too may want to have a really personal touch to your monogram, but if you are agonizing about what to do, choose something small, classic, and elegant, and you'll never go wrong.

MEN'S FUR STYLING

Fifteen percent of the fur-buying public is made up of men, who are getting more and more adventurous about furs. And while the rules and guidelines for buying and maintaining a fur are the same for men and women, there are a couple of tips that might let the balance of men overcome their reluctance to buy a fur. After all, men deserve the luxury, the glamor, and the warmth as much as women do.

The impact of a fur on a man is changed by the length and line of the coat. A full-length coat is very bold, but, according to Jeff Forman, of Goldin-Feldman, who sails through northern winters in a full-length tanuki, "There is no other coat that makes you feel as warm, as impervious to the elements, as bold. When heads turn, it is with envy. They are freezing and you are not!"

Men's coats are generally made of sporty, long-haired furs. Sleeker skins and trimmer styles are for the fashion iconoclast. Try on a beaver, raccoon, or tanuki. You'll be surprised by the power and attractiveness of the look.

If a jacket seems a more low-key statement, you can choose from a wider variety of furs. Coyote, lamb, fisher, and marten are all available. The jacket is most serviceable if it is long enough to be worn over a suit coat and full enough to allow for easy motion. Very sporty parka styles are even more widely available and will take you from the ski slopes to the theater.

The most common solution for men, however, is to own a fur-lined coat. If you buy a trench coat one size larger than usual, you can have a mink, sable, otter, opossum, or sheared nutria lining made for it. Fur on the collar may be just showy enough. That gives you the best of both worlds—the luxury and warmth of fur and the conservative look of a standard cloth coat.

Maintaining
Your Fur Coat

~

Once you have your fur coat, you want it to be a comfortable part of your life. Furs are not made to be hung in closets and keep your hangers company. They are made to be loved, worn, and enjoyed. There just aren't enough Saturday nights to justify buying a fur for only the most special occasions. All the precautions and instructions for the care and protection of the garment should not discourage you from enjoying it.

As I tell my customers, you can wear your coat as much as you like, but you must respect it. If you have a fine watch you can wear it every day, but you unconsciously change the way you move about, making sure you don't knock it against anything; you keep it out of water, and avoid getting it dirty. The same commonsense approach applies to maintaining a fur coat, and the rules you should follow do not really amount to more than a few easy-to-follow steps.

7

Caring for Your Coat

~

FROM THE MOMENT you bring your fur home, set up a simple routine for taking care of it. The proper hanger, the right amount of space in the closet, the right location—away from sunlight, heating units or ducts, and open windows—are all important. A furrier can, and should, assure you that when your coat leaves the showroom it meets the highest standards. I tell my customers that we stand behind the quality of the skins, the fur, and the construction; but this alone cannot ensure years of wearing pleasure. You can ruin your coat in one season if you are careless. Fur has two main enemies: heat and friction. Heat from radiators or sunlight; friction from lovingly stroking your coat or treating it roughly can cause major damage. One of the most recent problems we've seen is the effect of velour car seats on fur coats, especially in the shoulder-blade area. Unlike leather seats, which allow smooth, snag-free movement, the velour snarls the fur, knots it, and breaks it off. Another problem is caused by the fact that so many businesswomen carry shoulder bags and briefcases, which rub fur off along the sides of the coat and the tops of the shoulders. Obviously you can't give up carrying your papers, so you should make a conscious effort to alternate the side on which you carry your bag and try to avoid constantly rubbing against the fragile hairs.

Individual eccentricities can also damage your coat without you being aware of it. Recently a woman came into our showroom to complain that her coat was becoming worn along the left side. She felt it was a defect in the skins. I asked her to put the coat on and walk back and forth. What did I see? She pumped her left arm energetically as she walked and, without realizing it, she was the source of the problem.

There are some basic routines that everyone should adopt to keep a coat as beautiful as possible for as long as possible. As for your individual wearing style, try to become aware of how you move and how you treat your coat.

THE TEN FUR-CARE COMMANDMENTS

1. Always hang your fur coat on a hanger when you take it off. Use a wide, molded-plastic fur hanger that is curved forward. Place the front of the coat on the inside of the curve to protect the line of the shoulders and the drape of the coat.

2. Hang your coat in an uncrowded closet. Do not

squeeze it in, or the fur will become matted and flat.

3. Don't leave anything in the pockets—gloves, money, and so forth. The extra weight is hard on the shoulder seams and will make the pockets sag.

4. Turn the collar up to allow the hairs underneath to spring up and breathe.

5. *Never* store your fur in plastic or next to any garment in a plastic bag. The fur must be allowed to breathe.

6. Don't store your coat in a closet with mothballs.

7. Don't keep your coat anywhere near a drafty window. The excess humidity can be harmful and sunlight can speed the process of oxidation.

8. Don't spray cologne or perfume on fur. Alcohol will dry the leather and guard hairs.

9. *Never* brush or comb your fur. To revive it, shake the coat vigorously.

10. *Never* hang your fur near any source of heat or in sunlight. Light speeds the process of oxidation and can change the fur color over time.

SPECIAL HANDLING FOR LONG-HAIRED FURS

Long-haired furs are particularly delicate and should not be subjected to any extra friction or rubbing from other garments or from hangers. Be especially careful not to crowd your long-haired fur in a closet. After each wearing, vigorously shake out the fur to fluff it up. Never brush your fur. Do not sit on your long-haired fur while driving, at a concert, or anywhere else. If you can't take it off, then lift up the back of the coat and sit on your clothes. Wearing seat belts is especially hard on fur, so keep buckled up, but take your coat off.

SPECIAL HANDLING FOR SHEARED FURS

It is best not to allow your sheared fur to become wet. It cannot handle even a light rain as well as other furs and will easily become matted. Clean sheared furs annually to increase their life span.

THE DAILY REGIMEN

There are also basic do's and don'ts when it comes to wearing any fur coat. If you follow them you will double the life span of even the most delicate fur.

1. Beware of carrying shoulder bags when you wear fur. The hairs will break off in one season. Even the most durable minks suffer from this most common of all abuses.
2. Don't walk with your hands stuffed in your pockets. It will bruise the cuffs and the pocket openings.
3. Don't walk with a briefcase rubbing against one side of the coat. If you can't keep the briefcase away from the fur, at least alternate hands or carry it under your arms.

4. Always unhook or unbutton and lift up your fur or take it off when sitting on trains, buses, or in cars. This is particularly true of long-haired foxes and lynx.

5. Keep the fur firmly on your shoulders. Allowing it to slide around or slouch down in the back will produce avoidable wear spots and hurt the shape of the garment.

6. Don't wear a scarf around the outside of the neck. Place it inside the coat between your face and the fur. This keeps skin oils off the collar and prevents friction under the collar.

SPECIAL HANDLING FOR FURS IN RAIN

Stormy weather does not have to be bad news when you're wearing your fur. The guard hairs on natural minks and sables and on long-haired furs such as silver fox, raccoon, tanuki, fisher, and others are nature's way of fighting off the effects of rain and snow. You've never seen a mink with an umbrella! If the water is beading up on the fur, you're okay. However, a truly drenching rain, one that permeates the underfur and, heaven forbid, the leather, is not good for even the heartiest of furs. If the leather gets wet it will shrink, pucker, and misshape the coat.

One important warning: In a drenching rain don't take your coat off and turn it lining-side out. Not only will water spot and ruin the silk fabric, but the leather will be much more vulnerable through the lining than through the fur.

You can take care of your fur after it gets moderately wet. But if it becomes soaked to the leather, take it immediately to your furrier.

Avoid heavy rains. That sounds simple but it's not always possible. If the weather report is predicting heavy rains, don't wear your fur. If a hearty fur is caught in a moderate rain, do the following:

~ Shake out the fur immediately upon going indoors.
~ Place the fur on a hanger in a nonhumid room. Do not put a wet fur into a closed closet or any airless space.
~ Never, never dry your coat with a hair dryer or by placing it near any source of heat.
~ Once the coat sheds the moisture and the underfur is dry, reshake it and use the flat of your hand to gently fluff the hair against the nap. Shake it again.
~ If the rain has dampened the leather under the underfur, let it dry slowly and then take your coat to your furrier immediately. Let them do a professional job of cleaning and reviving the hairs. It's worth whatever it costs.

SPECIAL HANDLING OF SPOTS AND STAINS

By and large, you should not attempt to clean or repair furs yourself, because the risk of damaging the leather or the hairs beyond repair is too great. You cannot always get to your furrier right away, but there are some simple steps you can take. It is important that you follow them correctly.

~ When water or another clear liquid spills on your coat, blot it with a soft cloth or a tissue.

~ When a staining liquid such as red wine, coffee, or tea spills blot gently with a soft cloth, making sure you do not press the stain into the leather. Take your coat to your furrier as soon as possible.

~ Chewing gum can be removed by holding an ice cube against the gum until it freezes and loosens. Never pull the gum from the hairs, and don't allow the ice to melt into the leather.

~ Foods such as peanut butter, jelly, mayonnaise, and milk can be removed by using club soda and a soft damp rag. Always be very gentle. Take the coat to your furrier immediately.

SPECIAL HANDLING FOR FURS THAT SHED

As you have learned, some furs shed and some don't. If a fur sheds excessively, no matter what type it is, you should check with your furrier to see if there is a problem in the skins or in the way you are handling the coat.

Mink is not supposed to shed, but we once sold a mink that acted like a fox. The customer brought it back and we did what we could to remove all the loose hairs, but it still continued to shed. We realized there was something in the skins themselves that was causing this very rare problem (it's the only shedding mink I've ever heard of) and we replaced the coat.

At the other extreme, we sometimes get customers who

are upset when the fox or coyote or lynx that they have bought sheds. We can put the fur into a dryerlike machine, called a drum, which spins it around to try to minimize the initial shedding, but it cannot be eliminated forever. Long-haired furs shed; a regular gentle shaking can get rid of the loosest hairs, and proper summer storage helps control hair loss, but I don't advise wearing dark colors under any fox, lynx, or coyote because your clothes will look as if a cat climbed all over you. You can use a tape-lint brush right on the fur to remove excess loose hair, but be gentle.

One fifty-year veteran of the fur business, Henry Land-man, tells me that in the old days when a coat was finished the apprentice of the furrier would beat it for half an hour or more to shake off all the loose hairs. These days the machine finishing, drumming, and ironing are supposed to remove the small, free hairs that are stuck in the coat, particularly along the seams. Mr. Landman claims they don't do the job the apprentice used to, and sometimes even a mink can benefit from being manually rid of loose hairs.

EMERGENCY REPAIRS

There are some emergency repairs—those involving lining hems, pockets, and other finishing details—that you can do yourself. However, any repair work that involves the leather itself, such as small tears in the seams, should only be done by a furrier. Not only does the furrier have the proper equipment and skill, but he or she can also check the coat for any indications of other potential trouble spots.

Even missing buttons and broken closings should be

repaired by a furrier, who will know how to reattach them so they do not pull or rub.

You may walk around for a whole season with a button missing or a torn pocket, figuring you'll have it fixed when the coat is stored for the summer. You wouldn't walk around in a torn dress, so don't allow your fur to be treated with any less care.

STORING AND CLEANING YOUR FUR COAT

The single most important responsibility you have in maintaining your fur coat is to provide regular summer storage. From May to October, your coat should be given to your furrier for temperature- and humidity-controlled storage. If you miss even one summer you rob your coat of years of life.

Most furriers provide inexpensive storage for coats. Many places even have pick-up and delivery service, so there is no excuse for avoiding it. Yet many people just don't store their coat, and then they wonder why their once-beautiful fur looks like it's been stranded on a desert island. It has!

If you purchase a used coat or one at a caravan sale you can arrange with a local retailer to store your coat. Expect to be treated as attentively as if you had bought your coat from him or her. Maintenance is a large part of the retailer's business. When you take your coat in for summer storage, take advantage of the time to have major repairs and refurbishing done.

Generally speaking, most furs need cleaning every two years unless some disaster strikes that calls for immediate attention or if the coat has been worn very frequently. When a fur is cleaned it is also glazed. This is a simple ironing technique that increases luster and shine back to fading furs.

INSURANCE FOR FURS

Furs, like jewels, should be insured through a rider on your renter's or homeowner's insurance policy. Since furs are worn out of your home, you may need theft and damage protection as well. Ask the insurance agent the following questions: Does the policy replace a stolen fur at a depreciated value from the purchase price, or does it provide compensation for the cost of buying a replacement? Does the policy protect you from the cost of repairing damages? For example, if you are in a car accident and your coat is torn or damaged, will the coat be covered? Will the policy cover you when abroad?

Your furrier should provide a written appraisal. It is an official document that states your coat's value, the type of fur, the dimensions of the sweep and length, and the style of collar, cuff, shoulder, sleeve, and even monogram.

8

Repairing and Restyling Your Coat

~

I'VE SEEN COATS BURNED, cut with knives, caked with mud, worn down to the leather. They can all be saved if the basic skins are still healthy and beautiful. It's just a matter of patience and art. If your fur is worn with time or by some accident, or if you simply become tired of its styling or look, you need not toss it aside. Repairs and restyling can transform many of the most damaged or outdated furs. Fur can be replaced, long coats can be shortened, short coats can even be lengthened! There are few tricks that a master furrier cannot pull off if the basic fur is healthy and beautiful.

As a consumer you are faced with only one choice: Is this coat worth repairing or restyling, or is it time to let it go? There are many ways of refurbishing a fur. Once you are aware of the expense and effort involved, you can decide if restyling is the way to go, or if it's time to start all over again and begin the process of buying a new fur coat.

REPAIRING A FUR

After you have had your coat for several seasons it will inevitably become worn. The cuffs, pocket openings, hem area, and collar will show the effects of friction, skin oils, and time. On long-haired coats, particularly fox, guard hairs will break off and the underfur will show through. On minks and sables this shouldn't happen (if you've followed the maintenance guidelines) for at least eight to ten years. But many of us are careless enough to cause premature trouble spots to appear. There is no reason to be dismayed when this happens. A quality furrier is well able to make such problems invisible to the eye.

There are two distinct types of repair work that can be done: One type relies on simple tailoring tricks, which can disguise wear; the other requires major repairs and the use of new skins and is time-consuming and often expensive.

TOUCH-UP REPAIRS

It is very important that small areas of wear be fixed immediately. If you let them go, you will end up with a major, expensive repair job or, worse, no coat at all.

For minor repairs to small worn areas, it may not be necessary to replace fur with a new skin, which is a more expensive and major technique. Instead, the furrier should be able to offer solutions that depend on tailoring or the use of fur from some invisible area of the coat.

WORN CUFFS AND POCKET OPENINGS

Cuffs that are worn can have a turned-back cuff added or be turned under if the sleeve is long enough, and worn pocket openings can be repaired by turning under the fur. If the worn spots can't simply be turned under, sometimes we use extra fur from the hem or sleeve. This "borrowed" fur must match the color and texture of the area that is being restored. Only your furrier can decide if there is fur to spare on the coat and if the match will be convincing. Ask if it is a viable option when they recommend that you go the more expensive route that would replace the worn fur with a new skin.

Leather banding along the cuffs or pockets is another alternative. It should not compromise the look of even the fanciest fur; however, if a very wide strip of leather is required (over a half inch) it makes the coat look sportier, and you might want to consider fur replacement instead.

WORN COLLARS AND LAPELS

Collars and lapels, like cuffs and pockets, can often be fixed by simply turning the fur under to hide the wear spots. If the area is not too large this should not affect the fit or line of the coat. In many cases the area that needs to be disguised may be too large. Then it is preferable to have the collar restyled or to have it replaced by creating a whole new collar and lapel from new pelts or from a different variety of fur.

WORN HEMS

If your hem is worn you can have it turned up just a quarter of an inch. That is the simple and economical solution. If you don't want to lose even that much length, however, the only way to remake the hemline is take the whole coat apart and work new, matched fur pieces into the original construction of the coat. A true, but extreme example is the sable coat a customer wanted made one inch longer. The price: five thousand dollars.

SMALL FUR-REPLACEMENT WORK

If you want to have some fur replaced in your coat you will have to pay for a whole pelt and go through the time and expense of getting a perfect match.

However, if fur replacement is the only way to re-create the exact styling and look of a coat that you are not ready to abandon, then it offers the best results. Even cuffs or lapels that use only a little of the new fur can be ruined by a poor matching job. So respect your furrier's knowledge and art and let him or her do the job well. This is not something to be done during the winter months. The furrier needs the time to find the skin and do the repair well. Attend to such jobs during the summer while your coat is in storage.

MAJOR REPAIRS

The worst damage I ever saw to a coat happened when flaming cherries jubilee were spilled all over a lynx coat.

Every furrier has a tale of a coat that looked like an impossible repair job. Just recently a woman brought in a fisher coat. "There are three beers in here somewhere, I just don't know where," she said. On examining the leather under the lining we found a large area that was dried and slightly puckered. But even that was repairable, because the basic coat was healthy and beautiful. It isn't always that simple. When a coat has reached the natural end of its life, when the leather is dried and brittle so it tears like paper, when the seams will not hold up, or when large areas of fur have been worn down, it's time to let it go.

Only your furrier can evaluate the repairability of your coat. If he thinks it's a sound investment he can proceed. Have him provide you with a precise description of the area of the coat that will be replaced by new fur, an exact count of how many skins he will use, and a realistic estimated price.

You must understand that major repairs can e very labor intensive and costly. Since a matching pelt must be found, it can take quite a while. It is difficult to match the colors, particularly if the fur is dyed or oxidized. According to Larry Cowit, one of the finest matchers in the country, there are all kinds of ways to make a new skin match an older one. But it cannot be done properly by most furriers, and they need to have access to the best practitioners of the matcher's art. "Anyone can use us to obtain a perfectly matched fur. They just need to know we are here," Larry explains.

Major repairs, when large areas of fur are being integrated into an existent coat, call for a lot of refabrication work. The lining is removed, and all major seams are opened. The coat is renailed—just as it was after it had been let out and sewn into a pattern. The new pelt is prepared and let out, and then sewn into the coat as if the coat were being put together for the first time. All finishing work must then be redone and the coat fully reassembled. But when all this happens, it's like the phoenix rising from the ashes—or the cherries jubilee—and you've got your fur looking as good as new.

RESTYLING A FUR COAT

Restyling can be done because of wear and tear or it can be done simply because you're not having fun with your coat anymore.

You may have bought a sedate mink several years ago, but today you want something that is sportier or more fashionable. You may have gotten a second fur and simply want a coat to play in. You may have lost or gained weight or need the armholes lowered by the addition of a gusset. Or you may be hoping to get a few more years out of a coat that now is showing its age. Restyling may be the solution.

A coat is worth restyling if you don't care about the expense or if you feel that spending five hundred to fifteen hundred dollars to fix up what you have is more realistic than spending six thousand dollars on a new coat. These are very personal decisions, which only you can make.

A furrier can evaluate the condition of the coat. If the skins and leather are dry and brittle, or if the seams are giving out from age, he or she will recommend that you not restyle the coat. The furrier can also outline the styling options available without the additional expense of buying and inserting new pelts, or those options available if you choose to add new fur. The furrier can show you a coat on the rack that is an example of the new look you want. Don't be led blindly into a restyling.

A furrier should give you a written estimate of the cost of restoring the fur and break it down into labor and materials. A deposit will be required—refundable if the work does not satisfy you. Never pay in full before the work is done.

When it comes to restyling an older fur, there are four types of conversions that can be done. Let's take a look at each of them.

RESTYLING YOUR COAT INTO A JACKET

Many coats can be restyled into jackets with minor alterations to the shoulders and the back of the collar and by simply shortening the length. The addition of a belt across the lower back may add interest or help reduce fullness, but otherwise the look can remain the same. This is one sure way of getting matching fur for repairs to worn spots on the collar and cuffs.

You may want a new look, or you may feel the lines of the coat are inappropriate when the coat is shorter. You can change a full collar to a stand-up mandarin one or create an asymmetrical flat closing, instead of a notched, suit-style neckline.

You may even want to add, for example, silver fox trim to your mink. The artful combination of furs makes a stunning coat and is one way to completely alter the look; but be careful it doesn't look arbitrarily added on. If you're going to use replacement pelts to do the repairs, you might want to create this high-fashion look.

INCREASING THE SIZE OF YOUR COAT

If you like the new oversized look in furs or if you have gained weight since you bought your coat, you may want to change the line from tailored to expansive, which can be done with the addition of skins. Once again, the decision to spend the money to match the skins and have the coat resewn and retailored can only be made by you. The expense must be worth it to you; if it is, then don't hesitate to go ahead.

ADDING DETAILS

You may find that you wish you had a belt, cuff tabs, a half belt in the back, or different closings. These changes can do a lot to alter the impact of a coat.

CONVERTING AN OLD COAT INTO A LINING

Many people find the best way to restyle an older fur is to use it as a lining in a new coat. The fur is renailed to fit a precise pattern that is derived from the raincoat or wool coat you desire. Remember to buy your coat one size larger than usual for a comfortable fit. Long-haired furs do not make good linings; the best furs are mink, sable, otter, nutria, oppossum, and lamb.

There is almost no restyling job that cannot be done if the basic leather and hair are in good shape, and very subtle changes can make it seem as if you've gotten a whole new coat. Remember that a furrier can work magic; but he or she cannot make a new coat out of one that is at its natural limits of wear. Then it is time to begin the fun of shopping for a new one, all over again.

THERE'S NO TIME LIKE THE PRESENT...AND NO PRESENT LIKE A FUR

We have examined every aspect of buying a fur. You should feel confident about your ability to select the coat that fits your needs and suits your budget. There is no reason not to set out today to begin looking around at all the local fur stores and their selections.

If you have any other questions about furs, remember that the key is establishing a good relationship with a dependable, expert furrier. He or she will work with you to make your new fur the purchase of your dreams.

Index

~